THE NEW EAT YOURSELF THIN LIKE I DID!

QUICK AND EASY LOW CARB COOKBOOK

BY

NANCY MOSHIER, RN

DEDICATED IN LOVING MEMORY OF
MY MOTHER, PHYLLIS.

Published by
NANCY'S COOKBOOKS, INC. P.O. Box 338, Garrison, Mn. 56450
or visit us on our Website: www.low-carb-cookbooks.com

Printed at Gopher State Litho, Minneapolis, Mn. 55406 USA
Cover design by David Swanson

First printing.
Printed in the United States of America.

ISBN: 0-9701029-0-9

ACKNOWLEDGEMENTS

I want to thank the following people for all of their help in getting this cookbook completed. Thanks to my terrific husband Ron for all of his critiques of my recipes, and many, many hours of typing and designing the cookbook. (Although he never did turn down a sample!)

Thanks to my dear friend Jane Collen for believing in this project and for providing moral support and great ideas! Thanks to my parents for believing in me and my book and for being tasters (Guinea Pigs) along with my Aunt and Uncle, Bev and Chuck Mueller.

A big thank you to Chris and Robin Ashmore for giving me the idea to create this book in the first place. I'd also like to thank D.B. Shafer (Shaf) for all of his help with the computer and a great job on photography! And for the business end of this project I have been so fortunate to be dealing with great people. Thanks to Jay Perrill at *1st Scribe*, Jim Meyer, Steve Lange & Dave Swanson at *Gopher State Litho*, Mark Beiter at *Cardservices Int'l.* and Erik Haug at *Poste Haste*. I can't forget to thank Harold & Bobbie Gleason for getting us interested in the Atkins Diet in the first place.

And finally a special thanks to all of my many friends for ordering the cookbook before it was even printed. Now that's faith!!

Nancy Moshier

INTRODUCTION

I hope this cookbook will help those of you that need to lose weight but need some help with what to eat. This is not a diet book, but only a cookbook. Before starting, you need to decide which of the Low-Carb diets suits you best, buy the book, whether it be *Dr. Atkins New Diet Revolution, Sugar Busters, Carbohydrate Addicts Diet,* etc. then read it thoroughly.

The most important thing of all – you need to make the commitment to yourself that you are going to do this and stay with it! Then use these recipes as they fit with the amount of carbs you are allowed. My husband and I have found this to be the easiest way we have ever lost weight. My husband has been on maintenance since April '99 and I have been on maintenance since February 2000. We both know we will never gain the weight back.

We have made a lifetime commitment and you can too! You never have to go hungry again. Good luck to you and I hope my recipes help you to enjoy your journey to a slimmer and healthier life!

HELPFUL HINTS

I would like to help make your diet easier for you by providing the following hints.

Keep on hand:
- *Nancy's Ketchup*
- *Sweet Spicy Mustard Sauce*
- *Nancy's BBQ Sauce*
- *Nancy's Steak Sauce*
- *Salad Dressings*
- *Crushed Pork Rinds* (crushed in food processor and stored in airtight container.)
- *Jell-O* for quick snacks

Make ahead & freeze:
- *Cooked Italian Sausage* for pizza or frittata.
- *Tomato Paste* - measure 1 tablespoon and 3 tablespoon portions & wrap in plastic wrap, then put in lock-top bag.
- *Lemon, Orange & Lime Zest* – measure & wrap in plastic wrap, label then put in lock-top bag.
- *Appetizers – Ham & Spinach Drops, BBQ Meatballs & Teriyaki Chicken Wings* are just a few recipes that you can freeze ahead and have ready for a quick snack or for unexpected company!
- *Toast & chop nuts*, then freeze in lock-top bags.
- *Taco meat* – measure in recipe amounts and freeze in lock-top bags.

Make sure you always have food available for hunger attacks. Leftover sliced meats, French Deviled Eggs, Beef, Pork or Turkey salad is great on Romaine Leaves. Cubed or sliced cheese is handy for snacks. Pork Rinds and Salsa or Guacamole are also good – just watch the carbs in both of them.

HELPFUL HINTS

You can also make double batches to last several days when you are too busy to cook everyday. Some of the *Baked Breakfast Frittatas*, etc. can be re-heated for quite a few rushed mornings.

When you are invited out to friends for dinner, explain the diet you are on – true friends want you to succeed. If the menu is not on your program, ask if it's okay if you bring what you need to eat. If it's not okay, decline the invitation. If you go to a function with a set menu you cannot eat – eat before you go! And when dining out don't be afraid to ask for salad or cottage cheese instead of potatoes & bread. Most restaurants are very accommodating if you explain that you are on a low carb diet. I wish you all the best and hope I have been able to help you.

The carbohydrate counts on my recipes are accurate to the best of my knowledge. I have used *The Complete Book of food Counts by Corrine T. Netzer* and *Carbohydrates & Fat in Your Food by Dr. Art Ulene* as resources for carb counts. I also used the manufacturers carb counts on the labels on some of the products I used.

Nancy's Cookbooks

CONTENTS

TID-BITS

You may or may not have heard of *xanthan gum* and *guar gum.* These are thickeners and make a big difference in the recipes. They are a little expensive but last a long time. It takes very little of them for thickening and stabilizing certain foods. You can find these in a health food store. Remember that it doesn't take very much to thicken.

I also use Dr. Atkins Bake Mix in many of my recipes because it works well and is low in carbohydrates. Most health food stores have it and many supermarkets are starting to carry it.

If you can't find it at a store nearby, you can coder it from Dr. Atkins by calling: 1-800-6-ATKINS. Also, it's a little expensive but most recipes use small amounts so it lasts quite awhile.

If you want to make cheesecakes, it is most helpful if you purchase a 9" springform pan. Also, if you can find it in your area, Daikon radish makes a wonderful substitute for potatoes!

Enjoy! Bon apetit!!!

APPETIZERS & SNACKS

BBQ Meatballs

Servings: 32

1 pound extra lean ground beef

1/2 cup pork rinds, crushed, plain or spicy

1/2 cup water

1 large egg

2 cloves garlic minced or bottled fresh minced garlic (equivalent to garlic cloves)

1/4 cup onion, chopped fine

3/4 teaspoon salt

1/8 teaspoon black pepper

BBQ Sauce

6 ounces tomato juice (3/4 cup)

1 tablespoon brown sugar twin

1 1/2 teaspoons liquid smoke flavoring

Mix all ingredients (except BBQ sauce ingredients) well. Shape into 1 inch balls.

Bake in 1 layer in a 9X13 sprayed pan @ 350 degrees for 30-40 minutes.

Mix BBQ Sauce ingredients well. Set aside.

Remove meatballs from oven. Place in deep skillet. Pour BBQ sauce over and simmer over low heat 30 minutes covered.

*Makes about 32 outstanding meatballs with BBQ sauce @ less than a gram of carbs each!

Deep Fried Cajun Cauliflower

Servings: 4

2 cups cauliflower flowerets, 1" pieces

1 1/2 cups pork rinds, crushed fine (0 carbs)

1/4 cup + 2 tablespoons Dr. Atkins Bake Mix

3/4 teaspoon salt

1/2 teaspoon cajun seasoning, or season salt

1 large egg

1 teaspoon worcestershire sauce

1/2 teaspoon bottled fresh minced garlic, or 1 clove fresh garlic, minced

cooking oil, for frying (*Canola does not fry well)

Wash, dry and trim cauliflower and set aside. Heat cooking oil in deep fryer or heavy deep saucepan with candy thermometer to 375 degrees.

While oil is heating, mix pork rinds, Bake Mix, salt and cajun seasoning in a shallow dish. Set aside.

Beat egg, worcestershire sauce and garlic in a separate bowl. When oil is ready, dip caulifloweres, 4 or 5 at a time into egg, draining off excess, then roll in crumb mixture, shaking off excess.

Fry till well browned. Repeat till all cauliflower is used. Keep warm in 325 degrees oven on a paper towel lined pan till all is cooked.

Makes 4 delicious servings @ only 4 grams of carbs per serving!

Serving Ideas: *All other vegetable oils work well for deep frying.

Deli Meat Rolls

Servings: 24

8 ounces cream cheese, softened

1/2 large dill pickle, chopped fine and drained well

2 tablespoons onion, chopped fine

1/2 teaspoon garlic powder

8 slices deli roast beef, cut in 1/8" thick slices

Beat cream cheese till smooth with wire whip. Stir in remaining ingredients except meat. Mix well.

Spread evenly on meat slices, roll them up starting on the short side and hold in place with 3 evenly spaced toothpicks.

Slice each roll into 3 pieces. Serve immediately or cover and refrigerate.

Makes 24 appetizers @ .5 grams of carbs per serving. Wow!

Serving Ideas: You can use any kind of deli meat you like. Just make sure it has 0 carbs.

French Deviled Eggs

Servings: 16

8 large eggs, hard-cooked
3 tablespoons mayonnaise (0 carbs)
2 tablespoons Nancy's Red French Dressing (page 65)
dash salt

Cut eggs in half, lengthwise. Carefully remove yolks and place in a small mixing bowl. Mash yolks with a fork, add remaining ingredients and mix well.

Spoon evenly into egg white halves. Refrigerate.

*Makes 16 servings @ only a trace of carbs per serving!

Serving Ideas:
Sprinkle with paprika for nice presentation!

Guacamole

Servings: 18

1 cup ripe avocados, mashed (mash with fork, do not puree, should be lumpy)

1/2 teaspoon salt (scant)

1 teaspoon bottled fresh minced garlic, or equivalent fresh garlic, minced

1 teaspoon fresh lime juice (may substitute lemon juice)

jalapeno pepper, fresh, finely minced, seeded (optional)

Mix all together in small bowl. Cover with plastic wrap right against guacamole to prevent darkening.

Refrigerate until serving time.

*Makes about 18 - 1 Tablespoon servings @ 1.1 grams of carbs per serving.

Serving Ideas: Use on any of your favorite Mexican dishes, salads or use as a dip with pork rinds!

Ham & Spinach Drops

Servings: 18

1 tablespoon butter

1/4 cup onion, chopped fine

8 ounces cream cheese, softened

1 10 ounce package frozen spinach,, thawed and drained (squeeze out as much liquid as possible)

1 large egg

1/2 cup parmesan cheese, grated

1 cup ham, chopped fine or ground in food processor

1/4 teaspoon salt

pinch pepper

Pre-heat oven to 350 degrees. Place butter and onion in large glass bowl. Cover loosely and microwave 1 minute or saute' in medium saucepan over medium heat till onion is translucent but not browned.

Add cream cheese and mix well. Stir in remaining ingredients till well mixed.

Drop by tablespoons onto sprayed cookie sheet. Bake about 20 minutes or till set and bottoms are lightly browned.

Serve warm or cold. Refrigerate leftovers.

*Makes 18 appetizers @ only 1 gram of carbs per serving!

Serving Ideas: Also try using mini-muffin cups.

Sauerkraut & Ham Balls

Servings: 8

2 cups sauerkraut, drained and squeezed dry. (make sure that sauerkraut is no more than 1 gram of carbs per 1/4 cup.)

1 1/2 cups ham, chopped

2 ounces cream cheese, softened

4 ounces swiss cheese, shredded or cut up

1/4 cup + 1 tablespoon Dr. Atkins Bake Mix

1 large egg

1 large egg white

1/4 cup + 1 tablespoon plain or spicy pork rinds, crushed fine

1/8 teaspoon ground ginger

corn oil, for deep-frying

Place sauerkraut, ham and cheese in food processor and process till chopped very small. Add cream cheese and egg and pulse till well combined. Shape into 8 balls about 2" in size. Set aside.

Whisk egg white in shallow dish till foamy. In another shallow dish mix Dr. Atkins Bake Mix, pork rinds and ginger till evenly blended. Set aside.

Pour corn oil in deep fryer to line indicated on fryer and heat according to your fryer's directions.
*If you do not have a deep fryer, use a deep, heavy sauce pan and a candy thermometer. Heat oil to 375 degrees.

While oil is heating, roll each ball in egg white, shaking off excess, then roll in breading mix, shaking off excess.
Let set on waxed paper or plastic wrap while oil is heating.

Gently place in hot oil. Deep fry for 2 1/2 minutes till well browned. Do Not crowd and make sure oil returns to 375 degrees between additions.

*Makes 8 large fabulous Sauerkraut and Ham Ball servings @ 4 grams of carbs per serving!

Serving Ideas: Can also be served for a main dish.
VARIATION:
Reuben Balls - Substitute corned beef for the ham and proceed as directed. Serve with Nancy's 1000 Island Dressing (page 88) if desired. Also I use Vlasic Sauerkraut.

Sausage Stuffed Mushroom Caps with Pesto Cream Sauce

Servings: 10

10 large mushroom caps (1 1/2" diameter) wiped clean with damp paper towel

1 pound Roll of Turkey Store brand Hot or Mild Italian sausage

1 Recipe Pesto Cream Sauce (page 129)

Remove stems from mushrooms and save for another purpose. (Omelets, etc.)

Place mushrooms cavity side up on a sprayed baking sheet large enough to accommodate them in a single layer.

Divide sausage into 10 equal pieces and roll into balls. Place 1 sausage ball on each mushroom cap, pressing down slightly.

Bake @ 350 degrees for 45 minutes. Start making Pesto Cream Sauce about 20 minutes before mushrooms are done.

Arrange mushrooms on a serving platter, pour Pesto Cream Sauce over and garnish as desired.

*Makes 10 award-winning appetizers @ 3.2 grams of carbs per serving!

Serving Ideas:
*Sprinkle with fresh grated Parmesan cheese if desired.

Savory Stuffed Mushrooms

Servings: 9

9 large mushrooms, for stuffing (wipe clean and stems removed)

salt to taste

2 ounces sharp cheddar cheese, shredded

2 tablespoons onion, minced

1 teaspoon bottled fresh minced garlic, or equivalent fresh garlic, minced

1/2 of a 4 1/2 ounce can of ripe olives, drained and chopped

salt, to taste

Lightly salt cavities of mushrooms. Mix remaining ingredients in small mixing bowl. Divide evenly and stuff into mushrooms.

Place in a single layer on a sprayed baking pan. Bake @ 350 degrees for 25 minutes.

*Makes 9 terrific servings @ 1.5 grams of carbs per serving.

Serving Ideas:

*You can save the mushroom stems for another use. I often use them in many of my different egg dishes!

Smoked Sausage Appetizers

Servings: 16

1 1/2 pounds smoked sausage, fully cooked (make sure sausage is no more than 1 gram of carbs per 2 ounces) cut in 1/2" slices and remove casing

1/4 cup Nancy's Ketchup, found on (page 125)

2 teaspoons bottled fresh minced garlic, or equivalent fresh garlic, minced

1 medium onion, cut in 1" pieces (about 5 ounces)

1/2 medium bell pepper, red or green, cut into 1" pieces

1 tablespoon Brown Sugar Twin, sugar substitute

Saute' sausage cuts in a large, heavy skillet over medium heat, stirring frequently for 4-5 minutes or till beginning to brown.

Add onions and peppers and continue to saute' till onions are beginning to look translucent.

Add Nancy's ketchup, garlic and Brown Sugar Twin. Mix well and heat through. Keep warm till serving.

*Makes 16 appetizers @ only 2.3 grams of carbs per serving!

Serving Ideas: You can use both green and red peppers. Just use 1/4 of each pepper. Not only do they taste great together but they add lots of color to your dish!

Teriyaki Chicken Wings

Servings: 9

2 pounds chicken wings, disjointed and tips discarded
Nancy's Teriyaki Sauce
1/2 cup Kikkoman soy sauce (0 carbs)
4 tablespoons Nancy's Ketchup, found on (page 125)
4 teaspoons bottled fresh minced garlic, or equivalent fresh garlic, minced
1/4 cup + 1 tablespoon Sugar Twin, sugar substitute

Rinse wings and pat dry with paper towels. Place wings on a sprayed baking pan in a single layer.

Bake @ 400 degrees for 1 hour. Make sauce while wings are baking.

Mix all Teriyaki sauce ingredients together in a medium bowl. After wings have been in 1 hour, remove from oven and brush sauce all over wings. Return to oven 10 minutes. Heat remaining sauce till hot.

Place wings on serving platter or in bowl and pour remaining sauce over wings.

*Makes 9 - 2 piece servings @ only 1 gram of carbs per serving!

Serving Ideas:
If you like it hot, just add a little tabasco to give that zing!!

BEVERAGES

Chocolate Shake

Servings: 2

1 cup heavy whipping cream
6 - 8 ice cubes, cracked
4 tablespoons Sugar Twin, sugar substitute
1 tablespoon unsweetened cocoa
1/2 teaspoon vanilla extract

Pour cream into blender. With blender running on low, add Sugar Twin, cocoa and vanilla extract.

Turn blender to high and add ice cubes one at a time. Stop blender and scrape down sides if necessary.

Continue to blend till thick and creamy and ice cubes are completely crushed.

*Makes 2 delicious servings @ only 4.8 grams of carbs per serving!

Serving Ideas: VARIATION 1:

Strawberry Shake - Substitute 1/4 cup sliced strawberries for the cocoa, reduce Sugar Twin to 3 tablespoons and substitute strawberry extract for vanilla extract. Makes 2 servings @ only 4.8 grams of carbs per serving!

VARIATION 2:

Tutti Frutti Shake - Omit cocoa and vanilla extract, reduce Sugar Twin to 3 tablespoons and add 1/2 teaspoon each - banana extract, orange extract and coconut extract. Add 2 drops red food color. (optional) Makes 2 servings @ only 3.8 grams of carbs per serving!

Root Beer Float

Servings: 1
1 can sugar-free Root Beer (0 carbs)
1 frozen Whipped Cream Cloud, found on page (147)

Place whipped cream cloud in 12 ounce glass slowly pour Root Beer down side of glass.

Add a straw if you like and enjoy!

*Makes 1 very enjoyable serving @ only 1 gram of carbs!

Serving Ideas:

VARIATION:

Orange Dream - Substitute 1 can of sugar-free Orange soda (0 carbs) for the sugar-free Root Beer soda.
Add whipped cream cloud and enjoy. Tastes like a Dreamsicle!
Makes 1 very enjoyable serving @ only 1 gram of carbs!

Hot Chocolate

Servings: 2

1 cup heavy cream
1 cup water
1 tablespoon unsweetened cocoa
3 tablespoons Sugar Twin, sugar substitute

In a medium saucepan, heat cream and water till hot but not boiling.

Add cocoa and Sugar Twin and stir till dissolved.

*Makes 2 delicious servings @ 5 grams of carbs per serving!

Serving Ideas:

VARIATION:

For Mexican Hot Chocolate add a sprinkling of ground cinnamon!

BREADS

Butterscotch Pecan Muffins

Servings: 12

5 large eggs, separated
1/2 teaspoon cream of tartar
2 tablespoons water
1/2 cup heavy whipping cream
3 tablespoons butter, melted and cooled
2 tablespoons sugar-free Jell-O instant butterscotch pudding mix
2 tablespoons Dr. Atkins Bake Mix
2 tablespoons plain pork rinds, crushed fine
3 tablespoons Brown Sugar Twin, sugar substitute
2 teaspoons vanilla extract
3 tablespoons pecans, toasted and chopped fairly small

Place egg whites and cream of tartar in large mixing bowl and set aside. Place egg yolks, water, cream, butter and vanilla in another mixing bowl. Add pudding mix and beat with a wire whisk until fairly smooth. Add remaining ingredients (except egg whites) and whisk till well combined. Set aside.

Beat egg whites and cream of tartar with an electric mixer till stiff but not dry. Fold egg whites gently into yolk mixture till mostly blended. Use a gentle touch and DO NOT OVERMIX or egg whites will deflate. You will notice spots of white here and there and that's ok.

Spoon into 12 medium, well-buttered, non-stick muffin cups. Bake @ 350 degrees for 16-18 minutes. Cool 10 minutes in muffin tins before removing.

*Makes 12 incredible muffins @ 2.2 grams of carbs per serving.
Serving Ideas: Best when refrigerated and served cold.
*Great with Vanilla Butter or Maple Butter! Recipes found on page 128.

Garlic Poppyseed Rolls

Servings: 6

3 large eggs, separated
2 tablespoons butter
1/2 teaspoon cream of tartar
1/3 cup heavy cream
2 teaspoons Sugar Twin, sugar substitute
1/4 teaspoon salt
1/2 teaspoon baking powder
1 1/2 teaspoons bottled fresh minced garlic, or 3 cloves fresh garlic, minced
1 1/2 teaspoons poppy seeds
1/2 cup pork rinds (plain or flavored) crushed fine

Place egg whites in large mixing bowl, add cream of tartar and set aside. Melt butter in a medium microwave safe bowl for 15-20 seconds on high. Add remaining ingredients to melted butter (except pork rinds and egg whites) and beat till combined. Set aside.

Whip egg whites and cream of tartar till stiff but not dry. GENTLY fold in yolk mixture along with pork rinds. Do Not Overmix. Spoon evenly into buttered non-stick muffin or popover pans. Muffin cups will be full.

Bake @ 350 degrees for about 25 minutes or till browned. Cool in pans on a rack.

*Makes 6 rolls @ only 1.3 grams of carbs each roll!

Ham & Cheese Breakfast Muffins

Servings: 16

6 large eggs, separated
1 teaspoon cream of tartar
1/2 cup cottage cheese
1/4 cup Dr. Atkins Bake Mix
1 teaspoon salt
2 tablespoons green onion, minced
2 tablespoons butter, melted
1 teaspoon Sugar Twin, sugar substitute
2 cups ham (0 carbs)
1 cup cheddar cheese, cubed
1/4 cup cream

Place egg whites and cream of tartar in a large mixing bowl and set aside.

Place egg yolks in a medium mixing bowl. Add remaining ingredients in order given, mixing after each addition.

Whip egg whites and cream of tartar with electric mixer till stiff but not dry. Gently fold in egg yolk mixture. Divide evenly into 16 non-stick, buttered muffin pans.

Bake @ 350 degrees for 30-35 minutes.

*Makes 16 muffins to remember @ only 1 gram of carbs each!

Hush Puppies

Servings: 16

2 large eggs, separated
1/4 teaspoon cream of tartar
4 tablespoons green onion, include tops, chopped fine
1 teaspoon bottled fresh minced garlic, or equivalent fresh garlic, minced
1/4 cup whipping cream
1/4 cup water
1 teaspoon Sugar Twin, Sugar Substitute
1/2 teaspoon salt
2/3 cup pork rinds, crushed
1/2 cup Dr. Atkins Bake Mix
Oil for frying (do not use Canola oil - Best to use a deep fryer)

Heat oil to 375 degrees.

Place egg whites and cream of tartar in a medium mixing bowl. Set aside. Mix remaining ingredients, except pork rinds in a small mixing bowl and beat well. Set aside.

Beat egg whites and cream of tartar till very stiff. Stir egg yolk mixture into egg whites. Add pork rinds and beat till combined.

Drop mixture from a teaspoon into hot oil, fry about 3 minutes or till golden brown, turn once. Remove and drain on paper towels. Keep warm.

*Makes 16 Hush Puppies " to die for" @ only .8 grams of carbs each!

Serving Ideas:
"If you like them spicy, add minced, fresh Jalapeno pepper to taste!

Sour Cream Poppyseed Muffins

Servings: 12

5 large eggs, separated
1/2 teaspoon cream of tartar
1/4 cup heavy whipping cream
1/4 cup sour cream
3 tablespoons butter, melted
1 tablespoon sugar-free Jello instant vanilla pudding mix
2 tablespoons plain pork rinds, crushed fine
2 tablespoons DR. Atkins Bake Mix
1/4 cup sugar twin
1/8 teaspoon salt
2 teaspoons lemon zest, grated (only the yellow part)
1 teaspoon poppy seeds

Place egg whites and cream of tartar in a large mixing bowl and set aside. Place egg yolks in another large mixing bowl and add cream and sour cream and beat till combined. Add remaining ingredients in order given and beat well. Set aside.

Beat egg whites and cream of tartar with electric mixer till stiff but not dry. Fold egg whites gently into yolk mixture. DO NOT OVERMIX, some white streaks are alright.

Spoon into 12 medium, well-buttered non-stick muffin cups.

Bake @ 350 degrees for 20-25 minutes. Cool in pans for 10 minutes before removing.

*Makes 12 servings @ 1.2 grams of carbs per serving. Yummy!
Serving Ideas:
*Best when refrigerated and served cold.

Spice Doughnut Holes

Servings: 20

2 large eggs, separated

1/4 teaspoon cream of tartar

1/4 cup + 2 tablespoons heavy whipping cream

1/4 cup water

5 tablespoons Sugar Twin, sugar substitute

1/4 teaspoon salt

1 teaspoon ground cinnamon

1/4 teaspoon ground nutmeg

1/4 teaspoon ground ginger

1/2 teaspoon vanilla extract

1/2 cup Dr. Atkins Bake Mix

2/3 cup plain pork rinds, crushed fine

Cooking oil (do not use Canola)

Heat oil to 375 degrees in deep fryer. If you don't have a deep fryer you must use a candy thermometer to maintain temperature @ 375 degrees. Do not over-fill oil in fryer or it may bubble up.

Place egg whites and cream of tartar in large mixing bowl. Set aside. Place egg yolks in another large mixing bowl and add remaining ingredients, (except pork rinds) and beat well.

Beat egg whites and cream of tartar with electric mixer on high till stiff but not dry. Stir in egg yolk mixture. Add pork rinds and beat just till combined.

Drop by teaspoons into hot oil, fry 4 at a time until golden brown, turning only once. Drain on paper towel.
*Roll in a mixture of cinnamon and Sugar Twin if desired while warm.

Serve warm or at room temperature.

*Makes 20 Doughnut Holes @ .6 gram of carbs per serving!

Serving Ideas: "Remember if you don't have a deep fryer you need to use a candy thermometer to maintain temperature @ 375 degrees or your doughnut holes will be greasy.
Even taste great cold. Enjoy this treat!!

Strawberry Walnut Muffins

Servings: 12

5 large eggs, separated

1/2 teaspoon cream of tartar

1/2 cup heavy whipping cream

2 tablespoons boiling water

1 teaspoon sugar-free Strawberry Jell-O

3 tablespoons butter

2 tablespoons DR. Atkins Bake Mix

6 tablespoons Sugar Twin, sugar substitute, divided

2 tablespoons plain pork rinds, crushed fine

3 tablespoons walnuts, toasted and chopped small

1 teaspoon vanilla extract

1 cup strawberries , chopped

Place egg whites and cream of tartar in large mixing bowl, set aside. Place egg yolks in another large bowl. Set aside. Mix 2 tablespoons of Sugar Twin into strawberries and set aside.

Stir Jello into boiling water until dissolved then stir butter into Jello to melt. Add cream and mix well and stir into egg yolks. Add remaining ingredients, including remaining 4 tablespoons Sugar Twin (except egg whites and strawberries) and whisk till well blended.

Gently stir in strawberries. Whip egg whites until stiff but not dry. Gently fold strawberry mixture into egg whites. DO NOT OVER MIX!

Gently spoon into 12 buttered non-stick medium muffin cups. Cups will be full.

Bake @ 350 degrees for about 19 - 22 minutes. Cool in pan (they will fall some).

*Makes 12 servings @ 1.8 grams of carbs per serving without Nancy's Strawberry Spread and 2.5 grams of carbs with *Nancy's Strawberry Spread.

Serving Ideas: Best when refrigerated and served cold.
*Nancy's Strawberry Spread is found on page (128).

BREAKFASTS

Cauliflower & Ham Quiche

Servings: 6

2 cups cauliflower flowerets, 1" pieces

2 cups ham cubes (0 carbs)

1/4 cup green onions, sliced

1 1/2 cups cheddar cheese, shredded

1 cup Swiss cheese, shredded or cubed

8 large eggs

1/2 teaspoon salt

dash pepper

1 cup heavy whipping cream

Cook flowerets in boiling water till barely tender. Drain and rinse with cold water to stop cooking process. Drain and set aside.

Whisk eggs and cream in large bowl. Add remaining ingredients, including cauliflower and mix well. Pour into a 9" sprayed deep dish pie pan or equivalent baking pan.

Bake @ 350 degrees for 45-50 minutes or till just set. Let set at room temperature 5 minutes before cutting.

*Makes 6 servings @ only 4 grams of carbs per serving!

Serving Ideas:
*You don't have to be a big fan of Cauliflower to love this breakfast delight. It's delicious!!!
*Reheats well in the microwave!

Crustless Asparagus & Ham Quiche

Servings: 6

2 tablespoons butter
3/4 cup fresh asparagus, cut in 1" diagonal pieces
2 tablespoons onion, chopped
3/4 cup ham, chopped (0 carbs)
8 large eggs
1/2 cup heavy cream
1/4 cup water
1 teaspoon salt
1/2 teaspoon dry mustard
1 cup swiss cheese, shredded

Melt butter in 10" skillet over medium-low heat. Add asparagus and saute' for 3-4 minutes stirring frequently, then add onion and ham and continue to cook for another 2 minutes or till onion is soft.

Spoon into a sprayed 9" deep dish pie plate. Set aside.

In a medium bowl, whisk remaining ingredients together till light and fluffy. Stir in cheese. Pour over asparagus mixture in pie pan. Bake @ 325 degrees for 40-45 minutes or till set.

*Makes 6 incredible servings @ only 2.1 grams of carbs per serving!

Ham Hash & Eggs

Servings: 4

1 tablespoon cooking oil
1 tablespoon butter
2 cups ham, chopped small (0 carbs)
1/2 cup Daikon radish, or turnips peeled and shredded
1/4 cup onion, chopped
4 large eggs
salt and pepper, to taste

Heat a heavy, medium skillet on medium heat for 2 minutes. Add oil and butter, continue to heat till foaming subsides.

Add Daikon radish, cook and stir until radish is browned. Add ham and onion and fry until onion is translucent, or about 2-3 minutes, stirring frequently.

Spread mixture evenly in pan and make 4 rounded indentations with a large spoon. Slip 1 egg into each indentation. Cover and cook till eggs are desired doneness.

Serve immediately.

*Makes 4 servings @ 1.6 grams of carbs per serving using Daikon radish.
*Makes 4 servings @ 2.2 grams of carbs per serving using turnips.

Serving Ideas: Daikon radish makes a great potato substitute. Can be found at some grocery stores in the produce section.
It is a large, long white radish - looks like a huge parsnip. Very mild flavored!

Italian Frittata

Servings: 8

2 tablespoons olive oil

1/2 cup onion, chopped

1/2 cup fresh tomatoes, seeded and coarsely chopped

2 teaspoons bottled fresh minced garlic, or equivalent fresh garlic, minced

4 ounces Italian sausage, cooked and crumbled

10 large eggs

1/2 cup water

3/4 teaspoon salt

2 tablespoons ripe olives, sliced or chopped

1 teaspoon dried oregano leaves

1/2 cup cheddar cheese, shredded

3/4 cup parmesan cheese, preferably freshly shredded or grated

In a large, heavy, deep, oven-proof skillet with lid, saute' onions in olive oil over medium heat for 1 minute. Add tomatoes and garlic, continue to saute' just till onions are translucent. Remove from skillet and set aside.

Wipe out pan and brown sausage (or use thawed pre-cooked sausage and skip this step). Remove from skillet and set aside. Wash and dry skillet. Melt butter in skillet over low-heat, swirl to cover bottom of pan. Meanwhile, in medium bowl whisk eggs, salt and water till fluffy. Pour into skillet and cover.

When egg mixture on bottom starts to thicken, lift with spatula and let uncooked portion run underneath. When mixture is thickening, top with sausage, ripe olives, tomato mixture, cheddar cheese then parmesan cheese. Slide into preheated 325 degree oven to finish, about 13-15 minutes. Let stand 5 minutes before cutting.

*Makes 8 fantastic servings @ only 2.7 grams of carbs per serving!

Serving Ideas: I cook and crumble a lot of Italian sausage at one time. Measure and freeze it. Thaws quickly in microwave!

Pancakes with Maple Syrup

Servings: 14

3/4 cup Dr. Atkins Bake Mix

1/8 teaspoon salt

1 teaspoon ground cinnamon

2 tablespoons Sugar Twin, sugar substitute

1 cup water

6 tablespoons heavy cream

3 tablespoons cooking oil

3 large egg whites

1 teaspoon vanilla extract

MAPLE SYRUP

1/4 cup Brown Sugar Twin, sugar substitute

1/2 teaspoon Xanthan Gum

1 cup water

2 teaspoons maple flavoring

1 teaspoon vanilla extract

1/2 teaspoon Equal® sweetener

Whisk dry ingredients together in medium mixing bowl. Mix water, cream, egg whites and vanilla extract in 2 cup measuring cup or small bowl.

Whisk wet ingredients into dry ingredients till fairly smooth. Pre-heat griddle on medium heat. Pour from ladle onto lightly greased hot griddle or skillet into 4" pancakes.

Cook till edges are dry and many bubbles appear. Turn and cook till browned on other side.

MAPLE SYRUP - Mix Brown Sugar Twin and Xanthan Gum in small saucepan. Stir in remaining ingredients and heat over medium heat. Stir till hot and thickened.
Makes approximately 1 cup of Maple Syrup @ only 5.5 grams of carbs total!

*Makes 14 super pancakes @ only .9 grams of carbs per pancake without syrup!
*Makes 14 super pancakes @ only 1.3 grams of carbs per pancake with 1 tablespoon of syrup!

Pork Carnitas Frittata

Servings: 6

3 tablespoons butter, divided

1 1/2 cups pork roast or chops, cooked, (leftover works great) sliced thin in 1"X1/2" strips

4 tablespoons onion, chopped and divided

1 teaspoon bottled fresh minced garlic, or 2 cloves fresh garlic, minced

2 teaspoons fresh lime juice

12 large eggs

3/4 cup water

1 1/2 teaspoons salt

1/2 cup shredded cheddar cheese

1/4 cup cilantro leaves, chopped

1/3 cup fresh tomatoes, seeded and chopped

Saute' pork, 3 tablespoons onions and garlic in 2 tablespoons butter in small skillet over low heat. Saute' till onion is soft, about 3-4 minutes. Add lime juice and remove from heat and set aside.

Melt remaining 1 tablespoon butter in large, non-stick oven-proof skillet over medium heat. While butter is melting whisk eggs, water and salt together in large bowl till light and fluffy. When butter is bubbly, pour 1/2 of egg mixture into skillet. Cover and cook till eggs are set on bottom, (may still be runny on top).

Sprinkle pork mixture evenly over eggs. Carefully pour remaining eggs over pork, cover and place in pre-heated 350 degree oven about 12-15 minutes or till eggs are set. Remove from oven, sprinkle with cheese and return to oven till cheese is melted, approximately 7-10 minutes.

Remove from oven and sprinkle evenly with cilantro leaves, tomato and remaining 1 tablespoon onion. Let set 5 minutes before cutting.

*Makes 6 fabulous servings @ only 2.6 grams of carbs per serving!

Serving Ideas: Serve with salsa if desired but be sure to count the carbs in the salsa!

Puffy Baked Eggs

Servings: 12

18 large eggs
2 tablespoons butter
1 cup sour cream
1/2 cup heavy cream
1/2 cup water
2 teaspoons salt
1/4 cup green onion, sliced with tops
3 tablespoons Hormel Real bacon bits (in a jar)
1 cup cheddar cheese, shredded (1/2 of 8 ounce package)

Pre-heat oven to 325 degrees. Melt butter in 9X13 baking pan in oven for about 5 minutes.

Mix all ingredients well except green onion, bacon bits and cheese. Add onion, mix well and pour into prepared pan.

Bake about 35 minutes or until eggs are set. Sprinkle with bacon bits, then cheese. Return to oven until cheese is melted, about 5 minutes.

*Makes 12 incredible servings @ only 1.7 grams of carbs per serving!

Serving Ideas: Store in refrigerator. Keeps well for at least 5 days. Reheats well in microwave on medium. Makes for a quick breakfast to have on hand.
If your microwave only has High and Defrost, use Defrost until hot. High will make the cheese hard and rubbery!

Quick & Easy Tex-Mex Eggs

Servings: 2

1 tablespoon butter
1 cup Taco Meat, recipe found on (page 83)
6 large eggs
1/2 cup canned tomatoes with green chiles
3/4 cup cheddar cheese, shredded
salt and pepper, to taste

Heat 10" heavy, non-stick skillet over medium-low heat for 3 minutes. Add butter and swish to cover bottom of pan. Spread taco meat evenly in skillet and cover for 1-2 minutes to heat through.

Meanwhile break eggs carefully in small bowl. Gently pour over taco meat, taking care not to break yolks. Salt and pepper to taste.

Carefully spoon tomatoes and chiles over eggs. Cover and cook till eggs are almost done (to your liking). Remove cover, sprinkle with cheese and replace cover till eggs are done and cheese is melted.

Makes 2 tasty servings @ only 4 grams of carbs each!

Salsa Scramble

Servings: 2

6 large eggs
3 tablespoons water
1/4 teaspoon salt
1 tablespoon butter
3 tablespoons salsa (any kind with no more than 3 grams of carbs per 2 tablespoons)
1/2 cup cheddar cheese, shredded

Whisk eggs, water and salt in a medium bowl till light and fluffy. Heat 10" heavy non-stick skillet over medium heat for 2 minutes. Add butter and melt, spreading over bottom of pan.

When butter is bubbling but not brown, pour in egg mixture. Cook and lift and fold until eggs are nearly set.

Add salsa and continue cooking and lifting till eggs are set but moist.

Sprinkle with cheese, cover and turn off heat. Serve when cheese is melted.

*Makes 2 servings @ only 3.5 grams of carbs per serving!

Swiss Eggs & Sausage

Servings: 2

6 large eggs
1 tablespoon butter
4 tablespoons bell pepper, chopped, red or green
2 tablespoons onion, coarsely chopped
4 ounces fully cooked smoked sausage, sliced into 1/4" slices, remove casing (no more than 1 gram of carbs per 2 ounces)
2 slices swiss cheese (Kraft swiss in the long package)
2 tablespoons water
salt and pepper, to taste

Break eggs into medium bowl and set aside. Heat a heavy 10", non-stick skillet over low heat for about 3 minutes. Add butter and melt, spreading over bottom of pan.

Saute' peppers, onions and sausage till onions are translucent, about 3-4 minutes.

Lay cheese over mixture and cover till cheese melts. Remove cover and gently pour eggs over cheese, taking care not to break yolks. Cover and cook till eggs are done as desired.

*Makes 2 very generous servings @ only 4 grams of carbs per serving!

Taco Omelets

Servings: 2

6 large eggs

1/4 cup water

3/4 teaspoon salt

1 tablespoon butter

1 cup Taco Meat (page 83)

1/2 cup cheddar cheese, shredded

TOPPINGS (optional)

1 cup lettuce, shredded

1/2 cup tomato, chopped

1/4 cup onion, chopped

4 tablespoons salsa (no more than 3 grams of carbs per 2 tablespoons)

4 tablespoons sour cream

Whisk eggs with water and salt. Heat butter in an 8" heavy, non-stick skillet over medium-low heat. Add 1/2 of the eggs and cover. Remove lid and lift eggs, letting uncooked portion flow underneath till set. Spoon 1/2 cup taco meat on one side, then 1/2 the cheese. Carefully fold in half and place on plate.

Keep warm while repeating with remaining eggs, taco meat and cheese.

Top with any or all toppings.

*Makes 2 servings without toppings @ 1.8 grams of carbs per serving.
*Makes 2 servings with toppings @ 9.5 grams of carbs per serving.

Serving Ideas:
*Don't be afraid to add a little jalapeno or tabasco for some zip!

SOUPS

Chili

Servings: 4

1 tablespoon cooking oil

3/4 cup onion, chopped

2 pounds ground beef, lean, coarse ground if possible

3/4 teaspoon salt

1 tablespoon bottled fresh minced garlic, or equivalent fresh garlic

4 1/2 teaspoons chili powder

1 1/2 teaspoons ground cumin

1 cup tomatoes, canned, with juice

1 cup water

2 cups Daikon radish, peeled and cubed

Saute' onion in oil in 3 quart heavy saucepan on low heat till translucent, about 3 minutes.

Add ground beef and cook over high heat, stirring and breaking up with a spoon till browned and no pink remains.

Add remaining ingredients and simmer till Daikon radish is tender.

Serve with shredded cheddar cheese, chopped onions and sour cream if desired.

*Makes 4 servings @ 7 grams of carbs per serving without toppings.
*Makes 4 servings @ 11 grams of carbs per serving with toppings.

Serving Ideas:
*Toppings are figured on 1/4 cup of cheddar cheese, 2 tablespoons of onion and 2 tablespoons of sour cream per serving.

Cream of Broccoli Soup

Servings: 4

1 tablespoon butter

2 tablespoons onion, chopped

1 - 14 1/2 ounce can chicken broth

1 pound broccoli flowerets, trimmed and cut up

1 1/2 teaspoons salt

1 teaspoon garlic salt

1 cup heavy cream

1/2 teaspoon Xanthan Gum (thickener)

In a 3 quart heavy saucepan, saute' onions in butter over low heat till softened but not brown, about 3 minutes.

Add chicken broth and bring to a boil. Add broccoli, salt, garlic salt and reduce heat to low and cook covered till soft. About 15 minutes.

Add cream and heat through, Do Not boil. SLOWLY sprinkle in Xanthan Gum and stir till thickened. Serve hot!

*Makes 4 great servings @ only 5.7 grams of carbs per serving!

Ham & Asparagus Soup

Servings: 5

1 - 14 1/2 ounce can chicken broth

1/4 teaspoon salt

1 pound fresh asparagus, washed & trimmed into 1/2" slices

2 tablespoons butter

3 cups ham, chopped (0 carbs)

3 tablespoons onion, chopped

3/4 cup heavy cream

1/2 cup water

1/2 teaspoon Xanthan Gum, to thicken

Bring chicken broth to a boil over high heat. Add asparagus. Bring to boil again, reduce heat, cover and simmer till asparagus is tender, about 10-15 minutes. Remove from heat. Remove and set aside 1/2 cup asparagus. Place rest of asparagus and broth in blender container. Set aside.

In 3 quart saucepan, melt butter over medium-low heat, add onion and saute' till soft, about 2-3 minutes. Add ham and saute' another 3 minutes, stirring frequently. Add reserved 1/2 cup asparagus.

Blend remaining asparagus and broth till liquified. Add to ham, asparagus and onions. Add cream and water and continue to heat but DO NOT boil. Sprinkle with Xanthan Gum and stir briskly to thicken. Salt and pepper to taste. Heat another 2 minutes. Makes 5 1/2 cups.

*Serves 5 @ only 4.4 grams of carbs per serving. Super!

Oyster Stew

Servings: 3

1 pint oysters, fresh shucked with liquid
2/3 cup whipping cream
3/4 cup water
1 tablespoon butter
salt, to taste

Heat cream and water over medium heat in a medium saucepan till very hot but not boiling.
When beginning to get quite warm, add oysters to cream mixture . Heat oysters till edges curl - DO NOT OVER COOK or they will be tough.

Add butter and salt to taste.

*Makes 3 servings @ 8 grams of carbs each.

Serving Ideas:
A great recipe on a chilly day!

Turkey Egg Drop Soup

Servings: 6

3 cups turkey broth, leftover from roast turkey or turkey breast

1 - 14 1/2 ounce can chicken broth, ready to use - not concentrated

1/2 cup celery, chopped

2 large eggs, beaten

2 medium green onions, sliced with tops

salt and pepper, to taste

Kikkoman soy sauce, to taste

Cooked turkey, any amount cut in chunks - make it as meaty as you like!

Combine broths in a 3 1/2 quart saucepan, cover and bring to a boil over medium heat. Add celery and reduce heat to low, cover and cook till celery is tender. Increase heat to high, bring to a boil and slowly pour in beaten eggs, stirring constantly till eggs are set in shreds.

Add Turkey, bring to boil, then reduce heat to low and simmer 10 minutes. Season with soy sauce. Salt and pepper to taste. Start with soy sauce since it is very salty.

Add sliced green onions just before serving.

*Makes 6 servings @ 1.1 grams of carbs per serving!

Serving Ideas:
*You can try this recipe with leftover chicken. You'll be surprised how good it tastes!

SALADS & SALAD DRESSINGS

Cabbage & Bacon Salad

Servings: 6

1 - 1 pound head of cabbage, chopped small or shredded

1/2 medium bell pepper, red or green, chopped

3 tablespoons celery, chopped

1/2 cup cooking oil

1/3 cup rice vinegar

4 tablespoons Sugar Twin, sugar substitute

1/4 teaspoon dry mustard

1/2 teaspoon McCormick Onion Juice

1/2 teaspoon salt

1/4 teaspoon black pepper

3 tablespoons bottled Real Bacon Bits

Mix cabbage, peppers and celery in medium bowl with tight fitting lid. Mix remaining ingredients in a small bowl and pour over vegetables.

Mix well and refrigerate several hours to blend flavors.

*Makes 6 terrific servings @ only 4.2 grams of carbs per serving!

Confetti Salad

Servings: 5

1 - 14 1/2 ounce can French Style Green Beans , drained
1 cup fresh tomatoes, seeded and chopped
1/4 cup onion, chopped fine
6 large ripe olives, cut in thin strips
2 inch American cheese block (0 carbs), cut in 1/4" cubes
1/4 cup mayonnaise (0 carbs)
1/2 teaspoon Sugar Twin, sugar substitute
1/8 teaspoon salt
1/8 teaspoon pepper
5 cups lettuce, shredded

Toss all ingredients (except lettuce) gently together.

Makes 5 1/2 cup servings.
*Serve each serving over 1 cup shredded lettuce.
Refrigerate leftovers.

Makes 5 - 1/2 cup servings @ 5 grams of carbs each including lettuce!

Serving Ideas:

*Try using Romaine instead of head lettuce.

Creamy Cole Slaw

Servings: 10

4 cups cabbage, chopped fine

2 tablespoons red or green bell peppers, chopped fine

1/4 cup cream

3/4 cup mayonnaise

4 tablespoons Sugar Twin, sugar substitute

1/4 teaspoon salt

pepper, to taste

Mix cabbage and bell pepper together in a large bowl. Mix remaining ingredients together in a small bowl till smooth. Pour over cabbage and mix well. Chill in refrigerator.

Makes 10 - 1/2 cup servings @ only 1.8 grams of carbs per serving!

Dilled Creamed Cucumbers

Servings: 8

1/2 cup mayonnaise

1 1/4 cups sour cream

1 tablespoon Sugar Twin, sugar substitute

2 tablespoons rice vinegar

1 teaspoon dill weed

2 teaspoons bottled fresh minced garlic, or equivalent fresh garlic minced

1 teaspoon salt

5 medium cucumbers, peeled, sliced thin, salted well and drained in colander for 30 minutes.

Mix all ingredients (except cucumbers) in a medium size bowl. Rinse cucumbers well and pat dry with paper towels. Stir into dressing mixture.

Refrigerate and serve cold.

Makes 8 servings @ 6.5 grams of carbs per serving!

Serving Ideas:

Best if served chilled. Stores well in refrigerator.

Grilled Chicken Salad with Vegetables

Servings: 2

2 or 4 chicken breast halves, boneless

4 tablespoons olive oil, divided

garlic salt, to taste

1/2 medium red bell pepper, cut in 1" strips

1/2 medium green bell pepper, cut in 1" strips

1/4 medium onion, cut in thick strips

1 medium zucchini, sliced 1/4" thick

3 cups lettuce, any variety

1/2 medium tomato, cut into wedges

1/2 cup cucumber, sliced 1/4" thick

*DRESSING

1/3 cup olive oil

3 tablespoons rice vinegar

1 teaspoon Sugar Twin, sugar substitute

1/2 teaspoon bottled fresh minced garlic, or equivalent fresh garlic, minced

Wash chicken breasts and dry with paper towels. Brush both sides with 2 tablespoons of olive oil and sprinkle with garlic salt. Grill over medium coals or on gas grill. Turn every 2-3 minutes till juice runs clear. Keep warm.

Saute peppers, onions and zucchini in 2 tablespoons of olive oil in a medium size heavy skillet, till tender - crisp.
Sprinkle lightly with garlic salt while sauteeing. Remove from heat.

Arrange greens, cucumbers and tomatoes on 2 large serving plates. Arrange sauteed vegetables on top. Slice chicken and place attractively on salads. *Dressing - mix olive oil, rice vinegar, Sugar Twin and garlic. Drizzle over salads.

*Makes 2 servings @ 9 grams of carbs per serving!

Pork Salad

Servings: 10

1 pound pork roast, cooked, leftover
3 tablespoons onion, chopped
1/4 cup celery, diced
3/4 cup mayonnaise or sweet mayonnaise recipe found on page (67)

Place all in food processor and process till desired consistency.
Or chop roast, onion and celery fine by hand, then stir in mayonnaise.

*Makes 10 - 1/4 cup servings @ .4 grams of carbs each.

Roast Beef Salad

Servings: 7

1 pound leftover Roast Beef, trim fat and cut in 1" pieces
1/2 cup onion, coarsely chopped
1/2 cup celery, coarsely chopped
1 medium dill pickle, coarsely chopped
1 cup mayonnaise or Sweet Mayonnaise recipe (page 67)

Place roast beef in food processor bowl and chop into small pieces. Add remaining ingredients except for mayonnaise.

Process till desired consistency. Add mayonnaise and mix well.

If you don't have a food processor, you can grind meat in a grinder and chop remaining ingredients.

*Makes 7 - 1/2 cup servings @ 1.9 grams of carbs per serving!

Sweet Cauliflower & Bacon Salad

Servings: 10

1 medium head of cauliflower, cut into 1" flowerets

2 cups water

1 tablespoon salt

DRESSING

1/2 cup mayonnaise

1/4 cup whipping cream

2 tablespoons Sugar Twin, sugar substitute

3 tablespoons bell pepper (red or green), chopped

2 tablespoons onion, chopped fine

3/4 teaspoon salt

pepper, to taste

5 strips bacon, fried crisp, drained and crumbled or equivalent jarred Real Bacon pieces

Bring water to a boil in large sauce pan. Add cauliflower, then sprinkle with salt. Cover and bring to full boil again. Boil 1 minute, drain in colander, then return to pan and rinse in cold water till cool.

Drain and place in large mixing bowl. Set aside.

Mix mayonnaise and cream in small bowl till smooth. Add remaining dressing ingredients and mix.
Pour over Cauliflower and toss.

Refrigerate several hours.

Makes 10 - 1/2 cup servings @ 3.4 grams of carbs per serving!

Serving Ideas:
Real Bacon pieces are located in salad dressing aisle near the croutons.

Taco Salad

Servings: 2

4 cups romaine lettuce, coarsely chopped

2 cups Taco Meat (page 83)

1 cup shredded cheddar cheese

2 tablespoons onion, sliced thin lengthwise

8 cherry tomatoes, halved

4 large ripe olives, sliced

1/3 cup mayonnaise (0 carbs)

3 tablespoons salsa (no more than 3 grams of carbs per 2 tablespoons)

pinch of salt

2 or 3 sprigs of cilantro leaves, whole

sour cream (optional)

Arrange greens on 2 large plates. Top with taco meat, then next 4 ingredients in order given. Arrange attractively.

Mix mayo, salsa, salt and cilantro leaves. Spoon over salads evenly.

*Makes 2 servings @ 10 grams of carbs per serving!

Serving Ideas:
If you like it hot, add some tabasco or seeded Jalapenos.
*Be sure to count carbs in sour cream if used.

Turkey Salad

Servings: 6

4 cups cooked, leftover Turkey, chopped

1 stalk celery, about 9", chopped

2 medium green onions, sliced, including tops

3 tablespoons slivered almonds, toasted, (optional)

3/4 cup mayonnaise or sweet mayonnaise recipe for Miracle Whip Lovers (page 67)

1/4 cup heavy cream

salt and pepper, to taste

Mix all ingredients (except mayonnaise and cream) in a medium bowl. Mix mayonnaise and cream together in a small bowl till smooth. Pour over turkey mixture and mix till well combined.

Refrigerate covered.

Makes about 3 cups total.

*Makes 6 - 1/2 cup servings @ 1.8 grams of carbs per serving!
*Only .9 grams of carbs per serving without slivered almonds!

Serving Ideas: *Great spread on Romaine leaves!

VARIATION:

Chicken Salad - Substitute equal amount of cooked chicken for the turkey. Proceed as directed.

*For the best flavor, combine white and dark meat. You'll be amazed at how much better it is!!

Mediterranean Chicken Salad

Servings: 2

2 fresh boneless, skinless chicken breasts

2 tablespoons olive oil

salt and pepper, to taste

4 cups Romaine leaves, coarsely shredded

1/2 cup cherry tomato halves

2 ounces cream cheese, cut in 1/2" cubes

1/4 cup ripe olives, sliced

1/4 cup green onions, sliced in 1/2" lengths

1/2 cup *Sun Dried Tomato Mushroom Vinaigrette, page (66)

Wash chicken and pat dry with paper towels. Brush chicken breasts with olive oil on all sides. Salt and pepper to taste.

Grill or broil till juices run clear when pierced with a knife. Set aside to cool a bit.

On 2 dinner plates, attractively divide remaining ingredients in order given (except Vinaigrette). Cut slightly cooled chicken in slices or chunks and arrange on salads.

Drizzle with Sun Dried Tomato Mushroom Vinaigrette!

*Makes 2 simply super salads @ 9.8 grams of carbs per serving!

Bleu Cheese Dressing

2/3 cup mayonnaise

2/3 cup whipping cream

1/4 cup buttermilk

1 1/2 teaspoons bottled fresh minced garlic, or equivalent fresh garlic, minced

1/2 teaspoon garlic powder

1/8 teaspoon salt

1/2 teaspoon Sugar Twin, sugar substitute

1 - 4 ounce package crumbled Bleu Cheese

Mix all ingredients, except cheese, together in a medium bowl with a wire whip.

Stir in cheese. Pour about 1/2 of mixture into blender and puree. Stir back into remaining mixture and refrigerate.

Makes about 2 cups.

*1 Tablespoon = .4 grams of carbs per serving.

Ranch Dressing

1 cup mayonnaise
1 cup buttermilk
3/4 teaspoon Cavenders Greek Seasoning
1/4 teaspoon garlic salt, with parsley
1/4 teaspoon Sugar Twin, sugar substitute
few grinds of pepper
pinch Xanthum gum (optional for thickening)

Whisk all ingredients together till smooth and then refrigerate.

*Makes 2 cups @ only .4 grams of carbs per tablespoon!

Serving Ideas:

"Please remember that it only takes a small amount of Xanthan Gum to thicken a recipe!

Red French Dressing

Servings: 32

1 cup Hunts Tomato Sauce
1/4 cup white vinegar
1/2 cup + 2 tablespoons Sugar Twin, sugar substitute
2 tablespoons onion, chopped
1 clove garlic or equivalent bottled fresh garlic, minced
1 teaspoon dry mustard
1 cup cooking oil
pinch Xanthan Gum

Place all ingredients (except Xanthan Gum and oil) in blender container. Blend till onion and garlic are liquified.

While blender is running on medium speed, add oil VERY SLOWLY (1/8" stream) will take a few minutes. When oil is incorporated, continue blending another 30 seconds.

Add pinch of Xanthan Gum, blend a few seconds.

Refrigerate covered.

*Makes 3 cups of dressing.
* 1 tablespoon is only .4 grams of carbs!

Serving Ideas:
*Always shake dressing well before serving.

Sun Dried Tomato Mushroom Vinaigrette

Servings: 18

6 sun-dried tomatoes, (not in oil), snipped with scissors into small pieces

1/3 cup boiling water

1 - 7 ounce can mushroom stems and pieces, drained and chopped

3 cloves minced garlic, or equivalent fresh bottled minced garlic (do not use garlic powder or garlic salt)

1/2 cup extra virgin olive oil

1 cup canola oil

1/4 teaspoon salt

1/4 cup balsamic vinegar

1/4 cup white vinegar

1 tablespoon Sugar Twin, sugar substitute

1/2 teaspoon dried oregano powder

Mix all ingredients together and place in a covered container. Mix well before using each time.

Store in refrigerator.

*Makes 18 - 2 tablespoon servings @ only 1.2 grams of carbs per serving!

Serving Ideas:
*Refrigerates very well, just remember to stir before serving.

Sweet Mayonnaise for Miracle Whip Lovers!

1 quart mayonnaise (0 carbs)
1/4 cup Sugar Twin, sugar substitute

Spoon mayonnaise into medium mixing bowl. Stir in Sugar Twin till well combined.

Spoon back into jar and label SWEET.

*Makes 1 quart @ 0 carbs per serving.

Serving Ideas:
*Use in anything you love Miracle Whip in!

Thousand Island Dressing

1 cup mayonnaise

2 tablespoons whipping cream

1/4 cup Nancy's ketchup, found on page (125)

1 tablespoon dill pickle, chopped fine and well drained

1 tablespoon onion, minced

2 small pimiento, stuffed green olives, chopped

1 hard cooked egg, chopped fine

Combine all ingredients and stir till well mixed.

Store in refrigerator.

*Makes about 2/3 cup.

1 tablespoon = .7 grams of carbs per serving.

Serving Ideas:
*Not only is this dressing great on your favorite salad, but wait till you try it on the Reuben Balls found on page (16)!

ENTREES

Chicken Fried Steak

Servings: 3

2 pounds beef cube steaks

2 large eggs, beaten

3/4 cup pork rinds, plain or spicy, crushed fine

1 1/2 teaspoons seasoned salt

3 tablespoons Dr. Atkins Bake Mix

4 tablespoons cooking oil (Canola doesn't fry well)

salt and pepper, to taste

1 1/2 cups heavy whipping cream

1/2 teaspoon Xanthan gum (thickener)

Mix pork rinds, bake mix and seasoned salt in a large, shallow dish. Pie pan works well.

Beat eggs in another large shallow dish.

Dip cube steaks in eggs, then breading. Lay in 1 layer on waxed paper or foil.

Heat oil in large, heavy, non-stick skillet till hot but not smoking. Fry in 2 batches if necessary, adding more oil if needed. Keep warm uncovered in 225 degree oven. Pour off excess oil and add cream to skillet. Bring to boil, scraping any browned bits from bottom of pan. Sprinkle Xanthan Gum over and stir well till thickened.

Add salt and pepper to taste. Pour over steaks and serve.

*Makes 3 delicious servings @ only 5 grams of carbs per serving!

Ground Beef & Cabbage Casserole

Servings: 8

1 tablespoon cooking oil

1/4 cup onion, chopped

2 pounds lean ground beef

2 teaspoons salt, divided

1 teaspoon garlic powder

1 - 1 1/2 pound head of cabbage , cored and cut into about 1" pieces

2 tablespoons tomato paste

3/4 cup water

Saute' onion in oil over medium-low heat in a large, deep, heavy skillet about 2 minutes. Crumble ground beef into pan, increase heat to medium-high, add 1 teaspoon salt and garlic powder. Cook and stir till no pink remains.

Decrease heat to medium-low, add cabbage, remaining salt and tomato paste, mix well. Add water and mix well. Simmer, covered over low heat till cabbage is as done as you like.

*Makes 8 tasty 1 cup servings @ only 5 grams of carbs per serving!

Hamburger Mushroom & Green Bean Casserole

Servings: 5

1 teaspoon cooking oil

1/2 cup onion, chopped

1/2 cup celery, chopped

2 pounds lean ground beef

2 teaspoons garlic salt

1 teaspoon salt

1/2 teaspoon pepper

2 1/4 cups frozen green beans

3/4 cup heavy cream

1 - 7 ounce can mushroom stems and pieces, undrained

1 1/2 teaspoons beef bouillon granules, instant

1 teaspoon Zanthan Gum (thickener found at health food stores)

2 teaspoons Kikkoman soy sauce (0 carbs)

1/4 cup water chestnuts (sliced) cut in strips

In large deep heavy skillet, saute' onion and celery in oil over medium low heat, about 3-4 minutes till onion is tender. Add crumbled ground beef, garlic salt, salt and pepper, increase heat to high and brown, stirring often till no pink remains. Drain fat. Add green beans and reduce heat to low. Cover and simmer while preparing sauce.

Measure cream into bowl or large measuring cup. Drain mushroom liquid into cream. Add bouillon granules and mix well. Whisk in Zanthan Gum, then stir in mushrooms.

Stir into ground beef mixture and add soy sauce. Cover and simmer about 20 minutes or till green beans are as done as you prefer. Stir in water chestnuts and heat through.

*Makes 5 great servings @ 10 grams of carbs per serving!

Serving Ideas:
*Serve extra soy sauce on side.

Baked Italian Deli Sandwich

Servings: 4

4 large eggs, separated

1/4 teaspoon cream of tartar

1 tablespoon Dr. Atkins Bake Mix

1 tablespoon liquid from Marinated Artichoke Hearts

1/4 teaspoon salt

2 teaspoons bottled fresh minced garlic, or equivalent fresh minced

1 teaspoon dried basil leaves

1/4 teaspoon Xanthan Gum

1/4 teaspoon Guar Gum

1 pound Deli Italian Roast Beef, shaved, if unavailable use regular roast beef or cajun roast beef

1 - 6 ounce jar Marinated Artichoke Hearts

6 ounces hot pepper cheese, sliced

1/4 medium onion, sliced thin

Butter an 8" round or square cake pan. Place egg whites and cream of tartar in medium mixing bowl. Set aside.

In another medium bowl, whisk egg yolks and next 7 ingredients together. Set aside. Whip egg whites and cream of tartar till stiff peaks but not dry. Gently fold in egg yolk mixture. Pour 1/2 of batter into buttered pan.

Bake 10 minutes @ 350 degrees. Remove from oven and layer remaining ingredients in order given. Top with rest of batter. Bake about 25 minutes or till browned and springs back when touched with a finger.

*Makes 4 incredible servings @ only 7 grams of carbs per serving!

Meatballs Alfredo

Servings: 18

1 pound extra lean ground beef
1 pound Italian sausage (I use Jimmy Dean)
1/4 cup onion, chopped fine
2 teaspoons bottled fresh minced garlic, or equivalent fresh garlic, minced
1/2 teaspoon salt
1 large egg
1/4 cup plain pork rinds, crushed
1/2 cup water
1/2 teaspoon dried basil leaves
1/2 teaspoon dried oregano leaves
1 teaspoon fennel seed
pinch crushed red pepper
1 recipe *Nancy's Alfredo Sauce (page 121)

Mix all together (except for Alfredo Sauce) in a large mixing bowl with hands till well combined. Pat into a square on a piece of waxed paper or plastic wrap. Cut into 18 equal pieces and form each into a ball and place on a large sprayed baking pan with sides.

Bake @ 350 degrees for 45-50 minutes.

Make Alfredo sauce about 10 minutes before meatballs are done. Place meatballs in serving dish and pour Alfredo Sauce over meatballs and garnish with parsley if desired.

*Makes 18 delicious meatballs @ only 1.5 grams of carbs per serving!
Serving Ideas:
*Sprinkle with a little crushed red pepper for some excitement!

Mexi Stuffed Peppers

Servings: 6

3 medium bell peppers, green or red

2 pounds lean ground beef

1/2 cup plain pork rinds, crushed

2 large eggs

3/4 cup water

1 tablespoon bottled fresh minced garlic, or equivalent fresh garlic, minced

1/4 cup onion, chopped fine

1 tablespoon chili powder

2 tablespoons salsa, any kind (no more than 3 grams of carbs per 2 tablespoons)

2 teaspoons salt

1 1/2 cups cheddar cheese, shredded

Wash peppers, cut in half and remove seeds and veins. Mix remaining ingredients (except cheese) with your hands till well combined. Divide into 6 equal portions and stuff pepper halves with mixture.

Place in baking pan with sides, large enough to hold them in 1 layer. Pour 1/4 cup water in bottom of pan. Cover with foil and bake @ 350 degrees for 45-55 minutes or till cooked through.

Remove foil, sprinkle each with 1/4 cup cheese. Return to oven uncovered 10 minutes. Serve hot.

*Makes 6 generous servings @ only 4.7 grams of carbs each. Ole'!

Mexican Pizza

Servings: 18

MEXICAN PIZZA SAUCE

2 tablespoons tomato paste

2 tablespoons salsa

1/4 cup water

1 teaspoon garlic powder

1/2 teaspoon ground cumin

TOPPING

1 pound extra lean ground beef

3/4 teaspoon salt

1 1/2 teaspoons chili powder

1/2 teaspoon ground cumin

1 teaspoon garlic powder

1/2 cup ripe olives, sliced

6 whole jalapenos seeded, sliced and chopped (optional)

4 tablespoons onion, chopped

12 ounce package cheddar cheese, shredded

MEXICAN PIZZA SAUCE - Mix all ingredients together in a medium bowl and spread evenly on crust. Set aside.

TOPPING - Brown ground beef and seasonings in a medium non-stick skillet till no pink remains, breaking up with a spoon into small chunks. Drain well and spread evenly over crust. Top with olives, jalapenos, onions then cheese.
*Mexican Pizza Crust recipe found on page (77).

Bake @ 475 degrees for about 8-10 minutes.

*Makes 18 pieces @ 2.5 grams of carbs per serving!

Serving Ideas:
*If you don't like jalapenos you can leave them off.
*Also, if you make sure the seeds have all been removed they won't be as hot!

Mexican Pizza Crust

Servings: 18

3/4 cup Dr. Atkins Bake Mix

2 large eggs

1/3 cup heavy whipping cream

5 tablespoons water

1 teaspoon garlic powder

1 teaspoon chili powder

1/2 teaspoon ground cumin

3/4 teaspoon salt

2 large egg whites

1/4 teaspoon cream of tartar

1/4 cup plain pork rinds

Whisk all ingredients together, except egg whites, cream of tartar and pork rinds, in a large bowl. Set aside.

Whip egg whites and cream of tartar with electric mixer in a medium bowl till very stiff, but not dry. Fold egg whites into bake mixture.

Spread into sprayed 10"x15" jelly roll pan. Sprinkle with pork rinds.

Bake @ 350 degrees for 8-10 minutes or till just set. Cool for 5 minutes.

*Makes 1 Pizza Crust (18 servings) @ only .9 grams of carbs per serving!

Serving Ideas:
*Use for Mexican Pizza recipe found on page (78).

VARIATION:
Top Mexican Pizza Crust recipe with cheese, onions, black olives, jalapenos or any of your favorites and you now have yourself a Quesadilla! Just remember to count the carbs!

Old Fashioned Meatloaf

Servings: 8

2 pounds lean ground beef

3/4 cup water

1 teaspoon salt

1/2 teaspoon pepper

1/2 cup plain or spicy pork rinds, crushed

1 large egg

1 teaspoon bottled fresh minced garlic, or equivalent fresh garlic, minced

3/4 cup Nancy's Ketchup (page 125), divided

1/2 cup onion, chopped fine

Mix all ingredients including 4 tablespoons of ketchup together till well combined. You will need to use your hands. Shape into a loaf and place in a sprayed 9"x13" pan. Spread remaining ketchup on top.

Bake @ 350 degrees for 75-90 minutes or till done.

Makes 8 great servings @ only 2.5 grams of carbs per serving!

Serving Ideas:
"If you're a "Meatloaf Lover", this one's for you!

Pizza Roll Meatloaf

Servings: 8

2 pounds extra lean ground beef

1/4 cup onion, chopped

3 teaspoons bottled fresh minced garlic, divided or equivalent fresh garlic, minced

1 1/2 teaspoons dried basil leaves, divided

1 1/2 teaspoons oregano leaves, divided

1 teaspoon fennel seed

1/2 teaspoon crushed red pepper, divided (optional)

2 1/8 teaspoons salt

1/2 cup + 2 tablespoons water, divided

1/2 cup plain pork rinds, crushed

2 tablespoons tomato paste

1/4 cup parmesan cheese, grated

8 ounce package mozzarella cheese, sliced

1/2 cup fresh mushrooms, chopped or a 4 ounce can of mushroom slices, drained

1/2 cup pepperoni slices

Mix ground beef, onions, 2 teaspoons garlic, 1 teaspoon basil, 1 teaspoon oregano, fennel seed, salt and crushed red pepper if using, 1/2 cup water and pork rinds. Mix well for 1 minute.

Shape into a 10"x14" rectangle on waxed paper or aluminum foil. Set aside.

Mix tomato paste, remaining garlic, basil, oregano and remaining 2 tablespoons water. Spread evenly over meat. Sprinkle parmesan evenly over sauce, lay mozzarella slices over parmesan cheese. Top with pepperoni slices, then mushrooms.

Carefully roll meat from 10" side into a roll resembling a cake roll, using waxed paper or foil to help roll. Seal seam by pinching together well and seal ends by pinching together so cheese will not leak out.

Bake 1 hour @ 350 degrees. Let stand loosely covered with aluminum foil for 10 minutes before slicing into 8 equal slices.

*Makes 8 servings @ only 2.5 grams of carbs per serving.

Prime Rib with Mushroom Au Jus

Servings: 6

3 1/2 pound Beef Rib Roast, chine bone removed

1 tablespoon Schilling Montreal Steak Seasoning, regular or spicy

2 teaspoons bottled fresh minced garlic, or 4 cloves fresh garlic minced

1 double recipe *Marvelous Mushrooms (page 114)

Au Jus

2 cups beef broth or bouillon

1 teaspoon bottled fresh minced garlic, or 2 cloves fresh garlic, minced

1 tablespoon + 1 teaspoon Kikkoman soy sauce

2 teaspoons Worcestershire sauce (0 carbs)

Pre-heat oven to 325 degrees. Trim excess fat from outer edge of roast. Rub all sides with garlic, then sprinkle all sides with Montreal Steak Seasoning, pressing it into the meat. Place bone side down into sprayed roaster with at least 2" sides.

Roast until desired doneness. I use a meat thermometer and remove it from the oven when it is 5 degrees below desired temperature. If you do not have a meat thermometer, roast approximately 1 3/4 - 2 hours for Rare, 2 1/4 - 2 3/4 hours for Medium and 3 - 3 1/2 hours for Well done. A meat thermometer will indicate Rare, Medium and Well done.

While meat is roasting prepare *Marvelous Mushrooms.

When meat is at desired doneness, remove and place on cutting board and let stand for 15 minutes covered with aluminum foil before carving. While meat is standing, make Au Jus and add mushrooms. Heat till very hot.

Au Jus - Mix ingredients in a medium bowl and add to drippings in roaster. Bring to a boil, scraping browned bits from pan.

Slice roast and ladle Au Jus over each serving.

*Makes 6 wonderful servings @ only 5.4 grams of carbs per serving with mushrooms or 1.3 grams of carbs without mushrooms!

Serving Ideas: *You may omit mushrooms if you don't like them.

Quick Chow Mein

Servings: 4

2 pounds ground beef or chow mein meat (available at some supermarkets)

salt, to taste

1 teaspoon bottled fresh minced garlic or equivalent fresh garlic, minced

3 cups celery, sliced 1/3" thick

1/2 medium onion, sliced lengthwise (about 3 ounces)

1 cup beef broth or beef bouillon

1 - 7 ounce can mushrooms, sliced or stems & pieces, drained

1 - 8 ounce can bamboo shoots, drained, rinsed with water & drained

1 - 6 ounce can Dawn Fresh mushroom steak sauce (in a small yellow can usually found near bottled steak sauce)

3 tablespoons Kikkoman soy sauce

1/2 teaspoon Xanthan Gum

Brown ground beef or chow mein meat in a non-stick, heavy 4 quart saucepan over medium-high heat, breaking up meat with a spoon and stirring frequently.

When browned and no pink remains, drain fat and discard. Add celery, onions and beef broth and reduce heat to low, cover and simmer till celery is tender.

Add remaining ingredients and continue to simmer till heated through. Sprinkle Xanthan Gum over and stir till thickened.

*Makes 4 fabulous servings @ only 10 grams of carbs per serving!

Rueben Lasagna

Servings: 4

1 pound corned beef deli meat, sliced thin

8 ounces swiss cheese, sliced

1 cup sauerkraut (liquid squeezed out)

1/2 cup sour cream

2 tablespoons onion, finely chopped

1/4 teaspoon caraway seed (optional)

Mix sauerkraut and sour cream together. Spray 8" square baking pan. Layer 1/2 of corned beef on bottom. Cover with layer of cheese, then carefully spread 1/2 of sauerkraut mixture over cheese. Sprinkle with all of the onions.

Repeat layers ending with sauerkraut. Sprinkle with caraway seed if desired.

Bake @ 350 degrees for 35-40 minutes. Serve hot!

*Makes 4 large servings @ 6.9 grams of carbs per serving!

Serving Ideas:
*This entree is sure to please your guests!
Also, I use Vlasic sauerkraut.

Taco Meat

2 pounds lean ground beef
2 teaspoons garlic salt
2 tablespoons chili powder
1 teaspoon ground cumin
1 teaspoon salt

Brown ground beef over medium-high heat in a large deep skillet with remaining ingredients, breaking meat up with a spoon. When no pink remains, remove from heat and drain any excess fat. Cool slightly.

Use in Taco Salad (page 60), Taco Omelet (page 44) or Quick & Easy Tex-Mex Eggs (page 41).

*Makes approximately 7 cups.
*Whole recipe has a total of 7 grams of carbs.

Serving Ideas:
You can use your own imagination to create some wonderful entrees with this easy recipe!
*Freezes well!

Quick Hot Deli Plate

Servings: 2

1 pound Deli meat - shaved ham, roast beef, corned beef, pastrami, turkey or a combination of your favorite deli meats.
2 tablespoons green olives, sliced
2 tablespoons ripe olives, sliced
6 ounces cheddar cheese, swiss, hot pepper, mozzarella or your favorite, sliced

Divide all ingredients between 2 shallow soup plates sprayed with non-stick cooking spray. Layer in order given.
Cover each with sprayed plastic wrap or waxed paper. Microwave on medium until cheese melts.

*Makes 2 servings @ 6 grams of carbs per serving.

BBQ Ribs

Servings: 3

5 pounds pork spareribs, silverskin removed or at least cut through silverskin between the bones.

Brisket Rib (I use Adams brand)

1/2 cup *Nancy's BBQ Sauce (page 122)

Rinse ribs and leave damp. Apply brisket rub and rub into meat. It takes about 2-3 tablespoons or so.

Refrigerate in lock-top bag at least 8 hours. Preferably overnight.

Place ribs in single layer in large baking pan. Bake @ 300 degrees for 3 hours. Baste with BBQ sauce (page 122) the last hour.

*Makes 3 servings @ 3.7 grams of carbs per serving!

Serving Ideas:

*Serve extra BBQ sauce on the side if desired. Just count the carbs listed on Nancy's BBQ sauce recipe (page 122).

Fresh Pork with Sauerkraut Cabbage and Tomatoes

Servings: 6

2 1/2 pounds boneless pork top loin chops, or roast cut into 1/2" thick pieces

1 teaspoon cooking oil

6 slices bacon, cut in 1/2" pieces

1/2 cup onion, chopped

2 cups Vlasic Sauerkraut

2 1/2 cups cabbage, shredded

1 cup canned tomatoes, broken up with juice

1/8 teaspoon pepper

1 teaspoon Brown Sugar Twin, sugar substitute

1/4 cup water

salt, to taste

Heat large deep oven-proof skillet over medium-high heat, brush with oil. When hot, brown pork in a single layer on both sides. Remove to plate and set aside.

Lower heat and fry bacon for 2 minutes, add onions and continue frying till onions are translucent. Add remaining ingredients except pork, mix well and simmer over low heat till cabbage is limp. Add pork and bury it as much as possible in mixture.

Bake covered @ 325 degrees for 45 minutes.

*Makes 6 servings @ 6 grams of carbs per serving!

Serving Ideas: Watch for big difference in carbs between sauerkraut brands.

*Great with sour cream served on the side - just remember to count the carbs in sour cream!

Fried Smoked Sausage

Servings: 3

2 pounds smoked sausage (fully cooked and no more than 1 gram of carbs per 2 oz.)
1 large egg, beaten
1 cup pork rinds, plain or spicy - crushed fine
2 tablespoons Dr. Atkins Bake Mix
1/2 teaspoon garlic powder
1/4 cup corn oil

Remove casing from sausage and cut in 3" pieces. Cut each piece in half, lengthwise. Place egg in small bowl.

Mix pork rinds, bake mix and garlic powder in shallow dish. Heat oil in a large heavy skillet over medium heat.

When hot, dip sausage pieces in egg, then pork rinds and fry turning till browned on all sides.

*Makes 3 great servings @ only 6.3 grams of carbs per serving!

Serving Ideas:
*Pass Nancy's Ketchup, BBQ Sauce, Sweet Zesty Mustard or condiment of your choice. Just remember to count the carbs!

Ham Patties

Servings: 4

3 cups ham, ground - approximately 3/4 of a pound
2 large eggs
1/3 cup plain pork rinds, crushed fine
1 tablespoon prepared mustard (0 carbs)
2 tablespoons mayonnaise (0 carbs)
2 tablespoons butter

Mix all ingredients (except butter) together in a medium bowl. Melt butter on medium heat in large skillet till foaming subsides.

Shape mixture into 4 patties. Place in skillet and cook till browned. About 6 minutes, then turn and cook till browned on other side, about 7 minutes.

*Makes 4 terrific patties @ only .2 grams of carbs each!

Serving Ideas:
*Serve with Sweet Zesty Mustard Sauce (page 132) if desired.

Pizza

Servings: 15

1 recipe *PIZZA CRUST* (page 90)

PIZZA SAUCE

3 tablespoons tomato paste

1/2 cup water

2 teaspoons bottled fresh minced garlic, or 4 cloves fresh, minced

1 teaspoon fennel seed

1 teaspoon oregano powder

1/4 teaspoon salt

TOPPINGS

7 large ripe olives, sliced

5 fresh mushrooms, wiped clean with damp paper towel and sliced or use canned mushrooms

8 ounces Italian sausage, browned, broken up into pieces till no pink remains

3 tablespoons onion, chopped

1/2 cup parmesan cheese, grated

1/2 cup cheddar cheese, shredded

2 cups mozzarella cheese, shredded

PIZZA SAUCE - Mix all ingredients together in a small bowl. Spread evenly on pizza crust.

TOPPINGS - Spread toppings on evenly in order given.

Bake @ 425 degrees for 10-12 minutes or till cheese is melted.

*Pizza Sauce is .7 grams of carbs per serving.
*Makes 15 servings of Pizza crust, Sauce and Toppings @ only 2.6 grams of carbs per serving!

Serving Ideas: I buy the 16 ounce frozen Italian sausage rolls. Jimmy Dean and Turkey Store brands are low carb or use any brand that's low in carbs.

Pizza sauce can be used on any of your favorite recipes and it freezes very well! You can change the toppings as desired. Just adjust the carbs.

Pizza Crust

5 tablespoons Dr. Atkins Bake Mix

1/2 teaspoon salt

1 1/2 teaspoons Sugar Twin, sugar substitute

2 teaspoons dried oregano, leaves

2 teaspoons garlic powder

5 tablespoons parmesan cheese, grated

1/2 cup plain pork rinds, crushed fine (0 carbs)

1/2 cup water

1/4 cup heavy cream

2 tablespoons olive oil

1 large egg

Butter an 11"X15" non-stick, jelly roll pan. Pre-heat oven to 350 degrees. Whisk all ingredients together till well blended. Pour into pan and tilt bottom till evenly covered.

Bake about 12 minutes till set. Remove from oven and let cool 5 minutes. Turn oven up to 425 degrees.

Spread crust with pizza sauce, top with remaining toppings, ending with cheeses found on page (89).

*Makes 1 Pizza Crust equaling 15 pieces @ only .9 grams of carbs for each piece!
*Completed Pizza has only 2.6 grams of carbs per serving!

Pork & Cabbage with Sauerkraut

Servings: 4

1 - 1 1/2 pound head of cabbage, cut into 2" pieces
1/2 cup water
1/2 teaspoon salt
3 1/2 cups pork roast, cooked, leftover and coarsely chopped
1 cup sauerkraut, drained (I use Vlasic)
sour cream (optional)

Place cabbage and water in large saucepan. Sprinkle with salt. Cook over medium-low heat until limp.
Add pork and sauerkraut, continue cooking till cabbage is done to your liking.

Top with sour cream if desired.

*Makes 4 - 1 1/2 cup servings @ 8.4 grams of carbs per serving.

Serving Ideas:

*Sour cream is wonderful served with this dish, just be sure to count the carbs!

Pork Chops with Cream Gravy

Servings: 6

3 pounds pork chops

2 tablespoons cooking oil

2 1/2 teaspoons Old Bay seasoning

1/4 cup water or dry white wine

3/4 cup heavy whipping cream

1/4 teaspoon Xanthan Gum (thickener)

salt and pepper, to taste

Heat oil in a 12" skillet over medium-high heat till hot but not smoking. Brown chops in oil but don't over-crowd skillet. Brown in batches if necessary. Sprinkle with Old Bay seasoning while browning.

When all browned, reduce heat to lowest temperature and return all pork chops to skillet. Doesn't matter if they are layered at this point. Cover and cook 45 minutes or til tender. Check often and rearrange to cook evenly.

Remove chops to serving dish and cover with aluminum foil to keep warm.

Deglaze the pan with water or wine on medium-high heat, scraping browned bits from bottom of pan. Add cream, salt and pepper to taste. Bring to a boil, SLOWLY sprinkle Xanthan Gum over, stirring briskly. Simmer for 1 minute. Pour over chops and serve.

*Makes 6 incredible servings @ only 1.3 grams of carbs per serving!

Serving Ideas:
*This one is sure to please your taste buds!

Sweet & Sour Pork Vegetable Stir Fry

Servings: 4

2 tablespoons cooking oil

1 1/2 teaspoons bottled fresh minced garlic, or equivalent fresh garlic, minced

1 teaspoon chili paste (found in Oriental food section)

1/2 cup onion, sliced lengthwise

1 medium bell pepper, red or green, sliced in strips

8 ounces zucchini, cut in half lengthwise and sliced into 1/4" half-rounds

8 ounce can bamboo shoots, drained, rinsed and drained again

4 cups cooked roast pork loin, leftover, cut in 1/4" strips

1 tablespoon white vinegar

3 tablespoons chicken or beef broth

2 teaspoons fish sauce (found in Oriental food section)

4 teaspoons Kikkoman soy sauce

2 tablespoons Sugar Twin, sugar substitute

1/4 teaspoon Xanthan Gum

Heat a large heavy deep skillet or wok over medium-high heat for 1 minute. Add oil and swirl to cover bottom of pan and continue to heat for 1 minute. Add chili paste and garlic, stir for a few seconds. Add vegetables and stir fry for 2 minutes.

Add vinegar, broth, fish sauce, soy sauce and Sugar Twin. Then add pork and stir fry quickly to heat through. Add Xanthan Gum to thicken.

Serve immediately.

*Makes 4 incredible servings @ 7.1 grams of carbs per serving!

Serving Ideas: *This is a bit hot - if you don't like hot food you can omit the Chili Paste.

Zucchini Boats

Servings: 6

3 medium Zucchini, washed and ends trimmed and split in half, lengthwise

1 - 12 ounce roll Jimmy Dean 50% less fat sausage

garlic powder to taste

salt to taste

1/4 cup water

1 cup mozzarella cheese, shredded

1 cup cheddar cheese, shredded

Scoop seeds from Zucchini halves with a teaspoon and discard. Sprinkle scooped out cavities lightly with salt and garlic powder.

Divide sausage into 6 equal pieces and press into Zucchini Boats. Place in baking pan or large deep oven-proof skillet with lid. Pour water into bottom of pan and cover.

Bake @ 350 degrees for 45 minutes. Remove from oven and top with mozzarella and then cheddar cheeses.
Cover and return to oven for 5 minutes.

*Makes 6 servings @ 4 grams of carbs per serving!

Serving Ideas:
*Sprinkle servings with dried crushed red pepper if you like it hot!!

Chicken Cacciatore

Servings: 3

1 1/2 pounds boneless, skinless chicken breasts (or thighs)

2 tablespoons olive oil

salt and pepper, to taste

4 ounces fresh mushrooms, sliced or 7 ounce can drained

1/2 cup onion, sliced lengthwise

1 medium bell pepper, red or green, seeds removed and sliced lengthwise

1 cup canned tomatoes, with juice, cut into pieces

1 tablespoon tomato paste

1 tablespoon bottled fresh minced garlic, or equivalent fresh garlic, minced

1 teaspoon dried oregano leaves

1/2 teaspoon fennel seed (optional)

pinch crushed dried red pepper (optional)

2 tablespoons dry white wine (optional)

1/2 cup parmesan cheese, grated

1 cup mozzarella cheese, shredded

Brown chicken on both sides in hot olive oil, in a large heavy skillet on medium heat. Season with salt and pepper while browning. Remove from pan. Reduce heat and saute onions and peppers till onions are translucent, about 2 minutes. Add mushrooms and saute till limp, 2-3 minutes longer.

Add remaining ingredients except chicken and cheese. Bring to a boil, reduce heat to simmer and add chicken pieces, spooning sauce over. Add small amount of water if too dry.

Simmer covered about 20 - 30 minutes till chicken juice runs clear. Top each piece of chicken with cheeses, replace cover till melted.

*Makes 3 superb servings @ only 9.5 grams of carbs per serving!

Chicken Ole'

Servings: 4

2 pounds boneless, skinless chicken breasts or thighs (cut into coarse chunks)

1 tablespoon oil, for frying

salt , to taste

1/2 medium red bell pepper, sliced 1/4" x 1" long

1/2 medium green bell pepper, sliced 1/4" x 1" long

2 tablespoons onion, coarsely chopped

1 tablespoon bottled fresh minced garlic, or equivalent fresh garlic, minced

1 tablespoon fresh squeezed lime juice

2 cups cheddar cheese, shredded

Heat oil in large, deep, heavy non-stick skillet over medium-high heat. Brown chicken, sprinkle with salt, turning to brown both sides. Remove chicken to a plate and set aside.

Add onions and peppers to skillet and stir fry till tender-crisp. Return chicken to pan and add garlic. Reduce heat to very low, cover and cook 5-10 minutes or till chicken juices run clear. Watch closely so it doesn't burn.

Sprinkle with lime juice and mix well. Spread evenly in pan and sprinkle with cheese. Cover and remove from heat. Serve when cheese is melted.

*Makes 4 terrific servings @ only 3.5 grams of carbs per serving!

Chicken Parmigiana

Servings: 6

3 tablespoons olive oil

2 tablespoons butter

3 pounds boneless, skinless chicken breasts, rinsed, dried and pounded with meat mallet between sheets of waxed paper till 1/3" thick

1 recipe *Marinara Sauce* (124)

2 large eggs

1 cup plain pork rinds, crushed fine (0 carbs)

3/4 cup grated fresh Parmesan cheese, divided

2 tablespoons Dr. Atkins Bake Mix

8 ounces Mozzarella cheese, sliced

Beat eggs in shallow dish and set aside. Mix pork rinds, 1/4 cup Parmesan cheese and Bake Mix in a shallow dish or pie pan.

Heat olive oil and butter in a large non-stick skillet over medium-high heat till hot but do not let butter brown. When oil and butter are hot, dip breasts in egg, then in breading and fry till well browned on each side. Do in batches if necessary. Place on large baking pan and spread marinara sauce evenly over each piece.

Finish in 275 degree oven for 10 minutes. Top with remaining Parmesan and Mozzarella cheese. Return to oven for 5-8 minutes to melt cheese.

*Makes 6 incredible servings @ only 2.8 grams of carbs per serving!

Serving Ideas:
*This one is sure to impress your family and friends!

Quick Swiss Chicken & Broccoli Casserole

Servings: 6

1 medium head broccoli flowerets, washed (or substitute frozen)
1 tablespoon butter
2 cups fresh mushrooms, sliced (or use 7 ounce can, drained)
1/4 cup onion, chopped
3 cups cooked chicken, or turkey cut into coarse chunks
2 large hard-cooked eggs, sliced
4 ounces swiss cheese, shredded
3/4 cup mayonnaise (0 carbs)
1/4 teaspoon garlic powder (1/2 teaspoon if you prefer)
salt, to taste

In a large, deep oven-proof skillet, cook broccoli in small amount of boiling water, salted to taste, covered just till tender-crisp. Drain and remove to medium bowl.

Wipe out pan and melt butter in same pan over medium heat. Saute' onions till translucent, about 3 minutes.

Add mushrooms and continue cooking till mushrooms are limp. Stir garlic powder into mayonnaise. Return broccoli to skillet along with chicken or turkey and mayonnaise. Toss gently till combined.

Top with hard-cooked egg slices then cheese. Cover and bake @ 350 degrees for 30-40 minutes.

*Makes 6 very tasty servings @ only 4.7 grams of carbs per serving using fresh mushrooms!

Sweet & Sour Chicken

Servings: 4

1 recipe *SWEET & SOUR SAUCE* (page 131)
1 1/2 pounds boneless, skinless chicken breasts, rinsed, dried and cut into 1 1/2" pieces
2 large egg whites
1 cup plain pork rinds, crushed fine (0 carbs)
1/4 cup Dr. Atkins Bake Mix
1/2 teaspoon garlic powder
1/2 teaspoon ground ginger
oil for frying

Beat egg whites with a fork till foamy in a shallow dish. Set aside. Mix pork rinds, Bake Mix and spices in separate shallow dish.

Heat oil in deep fryer or heavy deep pan to 375 degrees using a candy thermometer. Dip chicken pieces in egg whites, then roll in breading, shaking off excess.

Fry till nicely browned and cooked through, about 2-4 minutes. Serve with Sweet and Sour Sauce.

*Makes 4 unbelievable servings @ only 1.1 grams of carbs without Sweet and Sour Sauce or 5.4 grams of carbs per serving with Sweet and Sour Sauce!

Serving Ideas:
    VARIATION 1:
*Sweet & Sour Pork - Substitute equal amount of fresh uncooked pork, cut in chunks for the chicken breasts. Proceed as directed.

    VARIATION 2:
*Sweet & Sour Shrimp - Substitute equal amount of peeled and cleaned raw shrimp for the chicken. Proceed as directed.

Broiled Halibut with Citrus Dill Butter

Servings: 2

1 pound Halibut steaks
3 tablespoons butter, softened
1/2 teaspoon lemon zest, grated
1/2 teaspoon dried dill weed

Place Halibut on a broiler safe pan. Mix remaining ingredients in a small bowl. Spread 1/3 of mixture on fish. Broil 5 inches from heat till fish is opaque and flakes easily with a fork. DO NOT over cook or Halibut will be dry. Time will depend on thickness of fish.

While fish is broiling, melt remaining butter mixture in a small saucepan and serve over Halibut.

*Makes 2 great servings @ only a trace of carbs per serving. Outstanding!!!

Serving Ideas:
*If you'd like you can use some of Nancy's Tartar Sauce recipe (page 133).

Crispy Fried Fish

*Fish fillets, any kind, rinsed
1/4 cup Dr. Atkins Bake Mix
1 teaspoon cajun seasoning, or season salt
1/2 cup pork rinds, crushed fine (0 carbs)
1 large egg
cooking oil

Pat fish dry with paper towels, set aside. Place baking mix, seasoning and pork rinds in a shallow dish or pie plate and mix well, set aside.

Beat egg in another shallow dish or pie plate. Heat 1/2" - 1" deep cooking oil in large, heavy skillet (or use deep fryer) till hot but not smoking. Temperature should be 375 degrees. If using a heavy skillet, use candy thermometer for best results.

Dip fillets in egg wash then dredge in breading. Fry till brown and just opaque inside. Should flake easily with fork. DO NOT OVER COOK. Servings depend on amount of fish prepared.

*Whole recipe of breading and batter is only 5.4 grams of carbs total!

Serving Ideas:
*Serve with Nancy's Tartar Sauce recipe (page 133).

Crusty Cajun Salmon with Cajun Mayonnaise

Servings: 2

1 pound Salmon fillet
1 tablespoon butter, softened
4 tablespoons pork rinds, crushed (0 carbs)
3/4 teaspoon cajun seasoning

CAJUN MAYONNAISE

3 tablespoons mayonnaise (0 carbs)
3/4 teaspoon cajun seasoning
1 teaspoon lime juice (can substitute lemon juice)

Rinse Salmon and pat dry with paper towels. Place in shallow sprayed baking pan. Spread butter over top.

Mix pork rinds and cajun seasoning and sprinkle over Salmon. Place in oven and bake @ 400 degrees till Salmon flakes with a fork and is opaque. DO NOT OVER BAKE or Salmon will be dry! Time will vary depending on the thickness of the fillet.

*CAJUN MAYONNAISE - Stir all ingredients together in a small bowl and serve with Salmon.

*Makes 2 magnificent servings @ only 1.9 grams of carbs per serving!

Serving Ideas:
   VARIATION:
You can substitute lemon pepper for the cajun seasoning and lemon juice for the lime juice.

Greek Baked Salmon

Servings: 2

1 1/2 pounds salmon fillet, rinsed and patted dry with paper towels
1/4 cup mayonnaise (0 carbs)
1/2 teaspoon Cavenders Greek Seasoning
1 teaspoon fresh squeezed lemon juice
1/2 teaspoon garlic powder

Place Salmon on a sprayed baking pan. Mix remaining ingredients and spread evenly over Salmon.

Bake @ 375 degrees for 25-30 minutes or till Salmon is opaque and flakes with a fork. DO NOT overbake.

*Makes 2 blue-ribbon servings @ only a 1.3 grams of carbs per serving!

Serving Ideas:
*Nancy's Tartar Sauce recipe (page 133).

Salmon Patties

Servings: 4

1 - 14.75 ounce can Salmon, drained, skinned and boned

3 tablespoons green onions, sliced (use green portion too)

2 tablespoons mayonnaise (0 carbs)

1 teaspoon dried dill weed

2 teaspoons fresh squeezed lemon juice (may use thawed Minute Maid lemon juice - but NOT lemonade)

1 large egg

1/2 cup plain or spicy pork rinds, crushed fine (0 carbs)

1/4 teaspoon salt

1/8 teaspoon pepper

3 tablespoons butter

Mix all ingredients together, except butter, in a medium bowl. Shape into 4 patties. Heat butter in a large skillet over medium heat till foaming subsides. DO NOT brown butter.

Add Salmon patties and cook for about 3 minutes or till golden brown, then turn and cook about 3 minutes longer or till golden brown.

*Makes 4 patties @ only .7 grams of carbs per serving!

Serving Ideas:
*You can serve this terrific entree with Nancy's Tartar Sauce recipe (page 133).

Shrimp Scampi Parmesano

Servings: 2

1 pound shrimp, raw fresh or thawed frozen, peeled and cleaned
3 tablespoons butter
1 teaspoon bottled fresh minced garlic, or equivalent fresh garlic, minced
1 teaspoon fresh squeezed lemon juice
2/3 cup parmesan cheese, shredded or grated
salt, to taste

Place shrimp in a sprayed baking pan with sides. Melt butter and mix with garlic, and lemon juice. Pour over shrimp.

Salt lightly if desired.

Broil shrimp just till shrimp turns pink and opaque. *Watch closely, it cooks fast!

Remove from broiler, sprinkle with cheese and return to broiler just until cheese melts.

*Makes 2 beautiful servings @ only 3.7 grams of carbs per serving!

Serving Ideas:
*Serve with lemon wedge if desired!

VEGETABLES

Baked "Potato" Casserole

Servings: 4

4 medium turnips, peeled, cut in 1 inch pieces. Rinse with water and drain.

2 ounces cream cheese (4 tablespoons)

1 tablespoon onion, chopped fine

1/2 cup cheddar cheese, shredded

Place turnips in medium sauce pan. Cover with water and add salt to taste. Bring to boil, reduce heat and cook covered till turnips are tender. Drain well and mash or whip with electric mixer. Add cream, butter, onion and mix well. Turn into a small buttered casserole dish.

Bake @ 350 degrees for about 35-40 minutes. Take out of oven and top with cheddar cheese and return to oven approximately 5 minutes or till melted.

*Makes 4 servings @ 8.3 grams of carbs per serving!

Cauliflower Scramble

Servings: 6

1 medium cauliflower head, washed and trimmed
2 tablespoons olive oil
3/4 teaspoon salt
1 Tablespoon bottled fresh minced garlic, or equivalent fresh garlic
1 large egg
2 Tablespoons whipping cream

Cut cauliflower into flowerets and slice into 1/8" thick slices, some will crumble and that's ok. Set aside.
Heat olive oil in a heavy, large, non-stick skillet over medium-high heat till hot but not smoking. Add cauliflower and salt. Make sure it is dry or it will splatter oil.

Beat egg and cream in a small bowl till blended and set aside. Cook and stir cauliflower about 5 minutes till somewhat browned but still tender-crisp. Stir in garlic and continue cooking and stirring about 1 minute.

Pour egg mixture over evenly and quickly stir to coat and cook till egg is set.

Serve immediately.

*Makes 6 servings @ 5.4 grams of carbs per serving!

Creole Green Beans

Servings: 7

1 pound fresh green beans, washed and trimmed
1/2 cup water
4 strips bacon
2 tablespoons onion, chopped
1/2 cup canned tomatoes, cut up
salt and pepper, to taste

Cook green beans in a medium saucepan with 1/2 cup water and salt to taste till desired doneness. Drain beans and set aside.

Fry bacon in 10" skillet until crisp. Remove from pan and drain on paper towels to remove excess grease.
Pour fat out of pan and saute' onions in frying pan till translucent.

Add tomatoes, beans and bacon. Heat through.

*Makes 7 - 1/2 cup servings @ 5 grams of carbs each!

Eggplant Parmigiana

Servings: 12

4 tablespoons olive oil

3 large egg whites

2 medium eggplants, about 1 pound each (washed and sliced into 6 even slices each)

salt

1 cup pork rinds, crushed fine (0 carbs)

1/4 cup Dr. Atkins Bake Mix

1 1/2 teaspoons dried oregano leaves

1 teaspoon garlic powder

SAUCE

1 cup tomato sauce (I use Hunts brand)

2 teaspoons dried oregano leaves

1 1/2 teaspoons garlic powder

1/2 teaspoon fennel seed (optional)

1 - 5 1/2 ounce can tomato juice (or 3/4 cup)

TOPPING

1/2 cup parmesan cheese, grated

1 1/2 cups mozzarella cheese, shredded

Place washed and sliced eggplant in a colander and heavily sprinkle all surfaces with salt. Let set for 30 minutes. While eggplant is setting, mix remaining ingredients, (except olive oil and egg whites) in a shallow bowl. Set aside. In another shallow bowl, beat egg whites with a fork till foamy. Set aside.

Rinse eggplant slices and pat dry with paper towels. Heat olive oil in a large, heavy, non-stick skillet over medium-high heat till a haze forms. Dip eggplant slices in egg whites, then into crumb mixture, shaking off excess. Fry till browned, about 4 minutes per side. Don't overcrowd. Fry in batches. When browned, place pieces on a large, buttered, non-stick baking sheet. If necessary use 2 baking sheets.

Mix all sauce ingredients, (except cheeses) in a medium bowl. Pour sauce over eggplant, top evenly with cheeses. Bake in pre-heated oven @ 350 degrees for 20 minutes or till eggplant is tender and cheese is melted.

*Makes 12 wonderful servings @ only 7.5 grams of carbs per serving!

Grilled Portobello Mushroom Caps

Servings: 2

2 Portobello mushroom caps

1/4 cup olive oil

1 tablespoon red wine vinegar

1/2 teaspoon oregano leaves

1 teaspoon bottled fresh minced garlic, or 2 garlic cloves, minced

1 tablespoon grated fresh Parmesan cheese

Mix all ingredients together (except mushrooms and cheese). Place mushrooms in quart size zip-lock bag, pour marinade over and close. Marinate 30 - 45 minutes.

Grill over medium coals or medium heat on gas grill for 2 1/2 minutes per side. Salt to taste. Sprinkle with Parmesan.

*Makes 2 servings @ only 4.4 grams per serving!

Ham & Swiss Green Beans

Servings: 5

1 pound green beans, fresh, trimmed or frozen
3/4 cup water
salt , to taste
1/2 cup whipping cream
1/4 cup water
3/4 cup ham, chopped in 1/4 dice (0 carbs)
2 ounces swiss cheese, cut in small cubes
1/4 teaspoon garlic powder
1/2 teaspoon Xanthan Gum, to thicken

Bring 3/4 cup water to boil in a 2 1/2 - 3 quart saucepan. Add salt to taste and green beans. Bring to boil again, cover, reduce heat and cook till desired doneness. Drain and discard liquid. Place into a serving bowl and keep warm. Covering them with foil will hold in heat.

Pour cream and water into same saucepan and heat over medium heat till hot but not boiling. Add remaining ingredients (except Xanthan gum) and stir till cheese is melted. Sprinkle Xanthan gum over and stir well till thickened.

Return beans to sauce and heat through.

*Makes 5 terrific servings @ only 7 grams of carbs per serving!

Italian Spinach

Servings: 4

10 ounces fresh spinach, pre-wash package

2 tablespoons olive oil

3 large cloves garlic, minced or bottled fresh, minced garlic

2 tablespoons onion, chopped

1/2 teaspoon dried basil leaves

1/2 teaspoon salt

4 tablespoons parmesan cheese, grated

pepper, to taste

Saute' onion in olive oil in large skillet over medium heat till soft but not browned. Add garlic, basil, spinach, salt and pepper.
Cook covered over low heat until very limp. Remove cover and cook till most of liquid is evaporated.

Divide into 4 servings and sprinkle each with 1 tablespoon of Parmesan.

*Makes 4 servings @ 3.9 grams of carbs per serving!

Marvelous Mushrooms

Servings: 3

1 tablespoon butter
8 ounces fresh mushrooms, sliced
1 teaspoon Cavenders Greek Seasoning
1 teaspoon bottled fresh garlic minced or 2 small cloves, minced
1/4 cup dry white wine
salt, to taste

Melt butter over medium heat in a small saucepan. Add mushrooms and saute, stirring frequently until mushrooms are limp. Stir in remaining ingredients (except salt) and bring to boil over medium-high heat.

Boil, stirring frequently till most liquid is evaporated. Add salt to taste. Yum!!

*Makes 3 servings @ only 4 grams of carbs per serving!

Serving Ideas:
*Serve on steaks or burgers for a great flavor combination!

"Potato" Latke Pancakes

Servings: 5

2 1/2 cups Daikon radish or turnip, peeled and shredded (find Daikon radish in produce section, may be near oriental vegetables)
1 large egg
2 tablespoons onion, chopped fine
1 tablespoon Dr. Atkins Baking Mix
1/2 teaspoon salt
butter, for frying

Mix all together in medium bowl (except butter). Heat butter on medium in large, non-stick skillet till foaming subsides. Drop by spoonfuls to make 5 pancakes using spoon to spread thin.
Cook over medium heat till underside is browned. Turn and cook till well browned and cooked through.

*Makes 5 Latke Pancakes @ 2.4 grams of carbs each with Daikon radish.
*Makes 5 Latke Pancakes @ 4.7 grams of carbs each with Turnips.

Serving Ideas:

*Try one of these delicious accompaniments:
1 tablespoon of unsweetened applesauce @ 1.5 grams of carbs.
1 strip of crisp fried bacon @ 0 grams of carbs.
1 tablespoon of sour cream @ .5 grams of carbs.

Sauteed Sesame Asparagus

Servings: 3

2 tablespoons cooking oil

1 pound fresh asparagus, washed well, dried and cut in 1 1/2" pieces, diagonally

1/2 teaspoon salt

2 teaspoons Kikkoman soy sauce

1 teaspoon sesame oil

Heat cooking oil in large, heavy, non-stick skillet over medium-high heat. Add asparagus, sprinkle with salt, stir and saute' till tender crisp.

Sprinkle with soy sauce and sesame oil and serve immediately.

*Makes 3 great servings @ only 3 grams of carbs per serving!

Sweet & Spicy Red Cabbage

Servings: 20

4 strips bacon

1 - 1 3/4 pound head of red cabbage , shredded

1 cup water

5 tablespoons red wine vinegar

3 tablespoons Brown Sugar Twin, sugar substitute

1/8 teaspoon ground allspice

1/8 teaspoon ground cloves

1 teaspoon salt

black pepper, to taste

Fry bacon in large deep skillet over low heat, turning frequently till crisp. Remove bacon and set aside. Crumble when cool. Add all remaining ingredients (except cabbage) to bacon drippings. Mix well and add cabbage and bacon.
Stir till combined. Cover and cook over low heat till cabbage is soft. Approximately 20 - 30 minutes.

*Makes 20 - 1/2 cup servings @ 4 grams of carbs per serving!

Serving Ideas:
*Store in refrigerator. Keeps well and reheats well.

Zucchini Alfredo

Servings: 4

2 tablespoons olive oil

3 medium-large zucchini, sliced 1/4" thick (total approximately 2 pounds)

1 1/2 teaspoons salt, divided

2 teaspoons bottled fresh minced garlic, or equivalent fresh garlic, minced

1/2 cup whipping cream

1 cup parmesan cheese, shredded

Heat olive oil in large non-stick skillet over medium-high heat. Add zucchini, sprinkle with salt and stir fry for 3 minutes. Add cream and garlic. Mix gently. Sprinkle with parmesan, turn heat off and cover till cheese melts.

Serve immediately.

*Makes 4 servings @ only 8 grams of carbs per serving!

Zucchini Italian Style

Servings: 6

4 medium zucchini, washed and sliced 1/4" thick (total approximately 2 1/2 pounds)

1/2 cup canned tomatoes, chopped

1 tablespoon tomato paste

1/2 teaspoon bottled fresh minced garlic, or equivalent fresh garlic, minced

1/2 teaspoon salt

1/2 teaspoon dried oregano leaves

1/2 teaspoon dried basil leaves

1/4 teaspoon fennel seed

1/2 cup Parmesan cheese

1/2 cup Mozzarella cheese

Toss all ingredients (except cheeses) together in a large bowl. Place in a sprayed baking dish sufficient size to hold. Cover with aluminum foil and bake @ 350 degrees for 20-25 minutes.

Remove foil, sprinkle with cheeses, return to oven for additional 10 minutes. Remove from oven and let stand 5 minutes. Cut into 6 servings.

*Makes 6 servings @ only 7 grams of carbs per serving!

SAUCES & CONDIMENTS

Alfredo Sauce

3 tablespoons butter

1 1/2 cups whipping cream

1/2 cup parmesan cheese

1/4 teaspoon salt

1 teaspoon bottled fresh minced garlic, or equivalent fresh garlic

Melt butter in a small saucepan over low heat. Add cream and stir. Add parmesan cheese and salt, stir and heat through. DO NOT boil.

Serve immediately.

Makes 1 3/4 cups @ only 1.7 of carbs per 1/4 cup serving!

Serving Ideas:
*Use over grilled chicken and steamed vegetables or stuffed mushrooms!

BBQ Sauce

Servings: 22

1 - 6 ounce can tomato paste

1 cup water

2 tablespoons white vinegar

2 1/2 tablespoons Brown Sugar Twin

1 tablespoon bottled, fresh minced garlic or equivalent fresh garlic, minced

1/2 teaspoon McCormick Onion juice

1/4 teaspoon liquid smoke flavoring (1/2 teaspoon if you like a smokey flavor)

1/4 teaspoon salt

1 teaspoon Worcestershire sauce (0 carbs)

Tabasco sauce, to taste (if you like it hot!)

Place tomato paste in a medium, heavy saucepan. Gradually add water, stirring well with each addition to smooth out lumps. Add remaining ingredients and simmer on low heat for about 15 minutes.

Store in refrigerator.

*Only 1.4 grams of carbs per tablespoon!

Serving Ideas:
*Serve over any of your favorite meats - like ribs, burgers, steaks or pork chops!

Berry Sauce

1 pint fresh berries
Sugar Twin, sugar substitute, to taste

Wash berries and place in a small saucepan. Add Sugar Twin to taste. DO
NOT add water, the water clinging to the berries is sufficient.
Cook over low heat, stirring frequently. Cook till syrupy and slightly
thickened.

Chill in refrigerator covered.

Total carbs for each recipe:

*BLUEBERRIES   56.8 grams of carbs total = 5.7 grams per tablespoon
*RASPBERRIES   36.1 grams of carbs total = 3.6 grams per tablespoon
*STRAWBERRIES 22.5 grams of carbs total = 2.5 grams per tablespoon
*BLACKBERRIES 36.8 grams of carbs total = 3.7 grams per tablespoon

Serving Ideas:
*Taste fabulous over cheesecake. Oh so good!!!

Marinara Sauce

1 tablespoon olive oil

2 tablespoons onion, chopped fine

2 teaspoons bottled, fresh minced garlic or equivalent fresh garlic, minced

1 - 5 1/2 ounce can of tomato juice

1 tablespoon tomato paste

1/4 teaspoon salt

1/8 teaspoon black pepper

1/4 teaspoon Sugar Twin, sugar substitute

1/4 teaspoon dried basil leaves

1/4 teaspoon dried oregano leaves

1/8 teaspoon fennel seed

*pinch of dried crushed red pepper (optional)

Heat olive oil in small saucepan over medium heat till hot and haze appears. Add onion and saute' for about 2 minutes. DO NOT brown. Add garlic and cook for 1 more minute. Add remaining ingredients and mix well.

Simmer for about 15 minutes over low heat.

Recipe contains only 13.2 grams of carbs total!

*Makes 5 servings - 3 tablespoons each @ only 2.6 grams of carbs!

Serving Ideas:
*Serve over steamed shredded zucchini, meatballs or grilled chicken breast. Mama Mia!

Nancy's Ketchup

Servings: 64

2 - 6 ounce cans tomato paste

4 tablespoons white vinegar

6 tablespoons Sugar Twin, sugar substitute

1 teaspoon garlic powder

1 teaspoon onion juice (McCormick brand)

1/8 teaspoon allspice

1/8 teaspoon salt

2 1/2 cups water

Mix all together in small saucepan and heat over low heat for 15 minutes to blend flavors.

Chill and store in refrigerator.

*Each Tablespoon contains only .8 grams of carbs!

Serving Ideas:
I put my Ketchup in a squeeze bottle to make it quick and easy to dispense!

Nancy's Pico De Gallo

Servings: 13

2 cups tomatoes, Roma tomatoes are best - cored, seeded and chopped into 1/4" dice

1 cup onion, chopped

1 teaspoon bottled, fresh minced garlic or equivalent fresh garlic, minced

1/2 fresh jalapeno pepper, seeded and minced very fine

1/2 teaspoon salt

1/4 cup fresh cilantro leaves, whole (usually found in produce section by the parsley)

2 tablespoons cooking oil

2 teaspoons lime juice

Mix all ingredients in a medium bowl.

Cover and refrigerate to blend flavors.

*Makes 13 - 1/4 cup servings @ only 2.6 grams of carbs per serving!

Serving Ideas:
Adjust the amount of Jalapeno to your taste or you can omit them if you prefer!
*Great with Pork Rinds or on Chicken Ole' (page 98).

Nancy's Steak Sauce

Servings: 22

2/3 cup Hunts Tomato Sauce

1 1/2 teaspoons Brown Sugar Twin, sugar substitute

1/4 teaspoon dry mustard

1/2 teaspoon turmeric, spice powder

1/2 teaspoon garlic powder

1 teaspoon McCormick onion juice

1 teaspoon cooking oil

2 teaspoons Worcestershire sauce (0 carbs)

3/4 cup water

1/2 teaspoon white vinegar

Mix all ingredients well and store in refrigerator.

*Makes 3/4 cup.
*1 Tablespoon serving @ only 1 gram of carbs!

Serving Ideas:
Using a squeezable bottle sure makes pouring quick and easy!

Nancy's Strawberry Spread

Servings: 10

2 tablespoons butter, softened

2 ounces cream cheese, softened

2 tablespoons heavy whipping cream

3 tablespoons Sugar Twin, sugar substitute, divided

1/4 cup strawberries, diced

Stir 1 tablespoon of Sugar Twin into strawberries in small bowl and set aside. Mix remaining ingredients in small bowl, add strawberries and mix well.

Refrigerate.

*Makes 10 - 1 Tablespoon servings @ only .7 grams of carbs per serving!

Serving Ideas: Use on Strawberry Walnut Muffins.

VARIATION 1:

*SWEET VANILLA BUTTER

4 tablespoons butter, softened

2 1/2 teaspoons Sugar Twin, sugar substitute

1/2 teaspoon vanilla extract

Mix all together in small bowl. Turn out onto plastic wrap and form into log, using plastic wrap to assist. Store in refrigerator. Slice off rounds as needed.

*Great on Sour Cream Poppyseed Muffins!   12 slices @ 0 carbs per slice!

VARIATION 2:

*NANCY'S MAPLE BUTTER - Just substitute 1/2 teaspoon Maple flavored extract for vanilla extract.

Makes 12 slices @ 0 carbs each! Maple butter is terrific on Butterscotch Pecan Muffins (page 28).

Pesto Cream Sauce

Servings: 6

3/4 cup heavy cream

1/4 cup water

2 tablespoons butter

1/4 cup prepared Pesto Sauce (found in refrigerated area in produce section)

1 teaspoon bottled fresh minced garlic, or equivalent fresh garlic, minced

1/4 teaspoon salt

3/4 cup parmesan cheese, shredded and divided

Heat cream and water in small, heavy saucepan over medium heat till hot but not boiling. Add butter, Pesto sauce, garlic and salt. Reduce heat and continue to heat about 5 more minutes on low heat.

Stir in 1/2 cup parmesan till melted. Use rest of parmesan cheese to sprinkle over top.

Makes 6 incredible servings @ only 1.9 grams of carbs per serving!

Serving Ideas:
*Serve over grilled meats or vegetables and your guests will rave!

Spicy Seafood Cocktail Sauce

1/2 cup *Nancy's Ketchup (page 125)
1 tablespoon prepared horseradish
1/2 teaspoon Worcestershire sauce (0 carbs)
1 teaspoon fresh squeezed lemon juice

Combine all ingredients in small bowl , cover and refrigerate.

Makes 9 1/2 tablespoons @ only .9 grams of carbs per Tablespoon!

Serving Ideas:
*Serve with any of your favorite seafood!

Sweet & Sour Sauce

Servings: 4

1 1/2 cups chicken broth

1/4 cup white vinegar

1/4 cup Sugar Twin, sugar substitute

1 teaspoon bottled fresh minced garlic, or equivalent fresh garlic, minced

1/4 cup *Nancy's Ketchup (page 125)

1 teaspoon cooking oil

1 teaspoon Xanthan Gum

1/4 of a medium onion, cut in 1" squares

1/8 of a medium red bell pepper, cut in 1" squares

1/8 of a medium green bell pepper, cut in 1" squares

Mix all ingredients together, (except Xanthan Gum, peppers and onion) in small saucepan. Bring to a boil and sprinkle Xanthan Gum in gradually, stirring constantly.

Add peppers and onions and reduce heat to keep warm.

Makes 4 incredible servings @ only 4.3 grams of carbs per serving!

Serving Ideas:
*Serve over Sweet & Sour Chicken, Pork or Shrimp (page 99)!
*Also great on grilled chicken or fish!

Sweet Zesty Mustard Sauce

Servings: 10

1/2 cup prepared yellow mustard (0 carbs)

2 tablespoons Brown Sugar Twin, sugar substitute

2 tablespoons *Nancy's Ketchup (page 125)

1 teaspoon prepared horseradish

1/4 teaspoon ground cloves

Mix all ingredients together.

Keep refrigerated and covered.

*Contains only .4 grams of carbs per tablespoon!

Serving Ideas:

*Makes an excellent glaze for ham. One recipe makes enough for a large bone-in half ham with enough left to serve as a condiment.

*Great sauce with burgers and hot dogs too!

Nancy's Tartar Sauce

Servings: 34

1 cup mayonnaise (0 carbs)
3/4 cup onion, grated with juice
2 tablespoons dill pickle, grated
3 tablespoons parsley, finely chopped
1 tablespoon fresh squeezed lemon juice

Place all ingredients in a medium bowl and mix well.
Keep refrigerated.

*1 tablespoon is only .4 grams of carbs!

Serving Ideas:
*Makes all your fish and seafood entrees that much better!

DESSERTS

Blueberry Dream Squares

Servings: 12

1 *Dessert Crust* (page 146)

Filling

2 - 8 ounce packages cream cheese, softened

1/4 cup Sugar Twin, sugar substitute

1/2 teaspoon Equal® sweetener

1 cup heavy whipping cream (whipped till thick, not stiff)

1 teaspoon sugar-free Jell-O instant vanilla pudding mix

Berry Layer

3/4 cup blueberries, fresh or frozen

2 tablespoons Sugar Twin, sugar substitute

Topping

1 cup heavy whipping cream

1 tablespoon sugar-free Jell-O instant vanilla pudding mix

1 teaspoon vanilla extract

*Make Dessert Crust and let cool.

FILLING: Mix cream cheese with electric mixer till smooth and fluffy. Add Sugar Twin, Equal and vanilla extract. Beat till blended. Set aside. Sprinkle pudding mix over whipped cream in medium bowl and stir in. Fold whipped cream into cream cheese mixture and spread evenly over crust. Make sure the crust is cooled first.

BERRY LAYER: Mix together and cook over low heat till syrupy. Cool. Spoon cooled berry mixture over filling. Refrigerate while making topping.

TOPPING: Mix all topping ingredients together and whip with electric mixer till very thick but not too stiff. Spread over berries. Refrigerate, covered.

*Makes 12 incredible servings @ only 5.4 grams of carbs per serving. Fabulous!

Serving Ideas:
*One of my husband's favorites!

Boston Cream Pie

Servings: 6

1 recipe *OLD FASHIONED VANILLA PUDDING* make ahead and
chill, (page 151)

1 recipe *CHOCOLATE GLAZE* make ahead and chill, (page 145)

1/2 cup Dr. Atkins Bake Mix

1 teaspoon Guar Gum

1 teaspoon Baking Powder

4 tablespoons Sugar Twin, sugar substitute

1 cup heavy cream

1/2 cup water

4 large eggs

2 teaspoons vanilla extract

1/2 teaspoon almond extract

Whisk Bake Mix, Guar Gum and Baking Powder together in medium bowl.
Add remaining ingredients and whisk till smooth.

Divide evenly into 2 well-buttered, non-stick, 8" round cake pans. Bake @
350 degrees for 22-25 minutes, till lightly browned and middle springs back
when touched with finger.

Cool in pans on racks for 5 minutes. Turn out of pans and finish cooling on
racks. Wrap with plastic wrap when completely cooled. Store in refrigerator
till ready to assemble.

*ASSEMBLY: Place 1 cake layer upside down on cake plate. Spread vanilla
pudding over top. Place second cake layer right side up over pudding layer.
Pour chocolate glaze over top and spread to run down sides. Chill till serving
time. Refrigerate leftovers.

*Makes 6 unbelievable servings @ only 7.4 grams of carbs per serving!

Serving Ideas: Cakes can be made a day ahead and wrapped in plastic and refrigerated.
*Assemble an hour or 2 before serving. Refrigerate till serving time.

Butterscotch Pecan Cheesecake

Servings: 16

1/2 cup pecans, toasted and finely chopped, divided

2/3 cup Brown Sugar Twin, sugar substitute, divided

5 - 8 ounce packages cream cheese, softened

1/4 pound butter, softened (1 stick)

1 cup heavy cream

1 tablespoon vanilla extract

1 small package sugar-free Jell-O instant butterscotch pudding mix

6 large eggs, yolks broken

butter for greasing pan

Grease sides and bottom of a 9" springform pan heavily with butter. Sprinkle 1/4 cup of pecans evenly on bottom, then sprinkle with 1 tablespoon of the Brown Sugar Twin. Cover sides and bottom with foil on the outside to keep from seeping. Set aside.

Beat cream cheese and butter in a large mixing bowl with electric mixer till smooth and creamy. Set aside.

In a medium mixing bowl whisk cream, vanilla, remaining Brown Sugar Twin and pudding mix. Mixture will become very stiff. Add to cream cheese, 1/4 at a time, beating till smooth with each addition. Add eggs all at once on low speed, just till incorporated. DO NOT OVER MIX or cheesecake will be grainy instead of creamy.

Pour into prepared pan and rap on countertop a few times to release air bubbles. Sprinkle remaining pecans on top.

Bake @ 325 degrees for 60-70 minutes or till just set. Turn off oven and leave inside for 1 hour. Take out and finish cooling at room temperature. Do Not Remove sides of pan till completely cooled to room temperature. Cover and refrigerate at least 6 hours before serving. Keep refrigerated. Will get firmer as it chills.

*Makes 16 incredible servings @ 5.4 grams of carbs per serving!

Cherry Cinnamon Dessert

Servings: 9

2 small packages sugar-free Jell-O, Cherry flavored

1 1/2 cups boiling water

2 cups cold water

1/2 cup unsweetened applesauce (1 single serving size small plastic container)

1 teaspoon ground cinnamon, and extra for garnish

1 recipe *Sweetened Whipped Cream (page 147)

Dissolve Jell-O in a 9" square or 7"x11" pan. Stir well until fully dissolved, this takes at least 2 minutes.

Stir in cold water and refrigerate until syrupy. Mix cinnamon into applesauce, then add to Jell-O, mixing well.

Refrigerate till firm. Spread whipped cream over top and lightly sprinkle with cinnamon.

*Makes 9 servings @ only 2.5 grams of carbs per serving!

Cherry Swirl

Servings: 12

JELL-O

2 small packages sugar-free Jell-O, cherry flavored

1 cup boiling water

3 cups cold water

CREAM CHEESE SWIRL

4 ounces cream cheese, softened

3/4 cup heavy whipping cream

1/2 cup water

2 tablespoons sugar-free Jell-O instant vanilla pudding mix

1 teaspoon vanilla extract

4 tablespoons Sugar Twin, sugar substitute

JELLO: Stir boiling water into Jell-O in a medium bowl till completely dissolved. Stir in cold water and refrigerate.

CREAM CHEESE SWIRL: Beat cream cheese in medium bowl till very smooth and fluffy. Set aside. Measure cream into a 2 cup glass measuring cup or bowl. Add pudding mix, Sugar Twin and vanilla extract. Whisk for 2 minutes still smooth. Whisk pudding mixture gradually into cream cheese mixture. Whisk in water. Set aside till Jell-O is syrupy - Do Not let Jell-O set up.

Pour Jello into a 7"X11" pan. Drop cream cheese mixture by spoonfuls over Jell-O and swirl by cutting through, back and forth with a knife. Refrigerate till set.

OPTIONAL: Add 1/2 cup canned drained sour pie cherries and 2 tablespoons Sugar Twin to Jell-O when syrupy. Continue as directed.

*Cut into 12 equal servings.   1.7 grams of carbs per serving without cherries and 2.8 grams of carbs with cherries.

Serving Ideas:
*Measure and freeze leftover cherries in Lock-top freezer bag.

Chinese Almond Cookies

Servings: 20

1/4 pound butter, softened (1 stick)

2 tablespoons peanut butter

2 large eggs

1/2 cup Sugar Twin, sugar substitute

1 teaspoon almond extract

1/2 teaspoon baking powder

1/8 teaspoon salt

1/2 cup Dr. Atkins Bake Mix

1/4 cup sliced almonds, toasted

In medium mixing bowl, mix butter and peanut butter together.

Add eggs, Sugar Twin, almond extract, baking powder and salt. Mix well. Stir in Bake Mix and almonds.

Drop from spoon onto a buttered cookie sheet, shaping nicely with a spoon. Bake 12-15 minutes @ 350 degrees.

*Makes 20 cookies @ only 1 gram of carbs per cookie!

Serving Ideas:
*Store loosely covered. Best when served warm.

Chocolate Almond Ice Cream

Servings: 12

2 1/2 cups + 2 tablespoons whipping cream, divided

12 ounces cream cheese, softened (1 1/2 - 8oz. packages)

3 Tablespoons butter, softened

3/4 cup Sugar Twin, sugar substitute

1 1/2 teaspoons vanilla

1/8 teaspoon salt

1/2 cup + 1 tablespoon water

1/4 cup sliced almonds, toasted

1 large package sugar-free Jell-O instant chocolate pudding mix (6 servings)

Whip 1 1/2 cups of cream with electric mixer in medium bowl till thick. DO NOT OVER BEAT. Set aside. Place cream cheese in large bowl and whip on high with same beaters till smooth. Mix in all remaining ingredients (except pudding mix and whipped cream) along with remaining unwhipped cream. Mix till just combined and smooth. Add pudding mix and whipped cream and mix on low speed till smooth.

Pour into 9x5x2 3/4" bread pan. Will be quite full or you can pour into 12 paper cups. Cover with plastic wrap.

Place into freezer till frozen all the way through. Usually takes overnight. Slice into 12 equal servings and cover leftovers.

*Makes 12 fantastic servings @ 7 grams of carbs per serving!

Serving Ideas:
*Place in microwave on low for 15 seconds to soften.

Chocolate Cheesecake

Servings: 16

5 - 8 ounce packages cream cheese, softened

1/4 pound butter, softened (1 stick)

1 cup heavy whipping cream

2 teaspoons vanilla

3/4 cup Sugar Twin, sugar substitute

1 - 1.4 ounce package sugar-free Jell-O instant chocolate pudding mix

2 - 1 ounce squares unsweetened baking chocolate, melted

6 large eggs, yolks broken

Beat cream cheese and butter in large mixing bowl till smooth and fluffy. Set aside. In medium mixing bowl, whisk cream, vanilla, Sugar Twin, melted chocolate and pudding mix. Mixture will become VERY stiff. Add to cream cheese, 1/4 at a time and beat till smooth. When all is smooth, add eggs all at once. Mix on low speed JUST till eggs are incorporated. DO NOT OVER MIX or texture will be grainy instead of creamy!

Spray a 9" springform pan and cover outside bottom and sides with aluminum foil. Pour mixture into pan and rap on countertop a few times to release air bubbles.

Bake @ 325 degrees for 60 to 70 minutes or until just set. Then turn oven off and leave in 1 additional hour. Finish cooling at room temperature. Do Not Remove sides of pan until completely cooled to room temperature. Cover and refrigerate at least 6 hours. Will get firmer as it chills.

*Makes 16 terrific servings @ 6.4 grams of carbs per serving!

Serving Ideas: "This one is for all the "Chocolate Lovers" out there!

Chocolate Cupcakes

Servings: 18

4 large eggs, separated

3/4 teaspoon cream of tartar

1 - 2.1 ounce package sugar-free Jell-O instant chocolate pudding mix (6 serving size), divided (save the remaining pudding mix for frosting, page 144)

1/2 cup water

1/2 cup Sugar Twin, sugar substitute

1 teaspoon baking powder

1/2 cup heavy cream

1 teaspoon vanilla extract

Pre-heat oven to 350 degrees.
Place egg whites and cream of tartar in medium mixing bowl and set aside. Measure out 6 tablespoons of pudding mix and set aside. Mix cream and water in a large bowl. Add Sugar Twin, baking powder, vanilla extract and the 6 tablespoons of pudding mix and beat till smooth. Set aside.

Whip egg whites and cream of tartar with electric mixer till stiff but not dry. Gently fold chocolate mixture into egg whites. Divide evenly into 18 buttered, non-stick mini muffin pans. Bake @ 350 degrees for 18-20 minutes. Cool in pans. They will collapse some.

*When cool, frost with Chocolate Cream Frosting (page 144). Refrigerate till cold.

*Makes 18 fabulous Chocolate Cupcakes @ only 5.5 grams of carbs each, frosted and 4 grams of carbs without frosting!

Serving Ideas: *Taste the best when cold!*

Chocolate Cream Frosting

Servings: 18

1/2 cup whipping cream, whipped till thick
4 ounces cream cheese, softened
1 tablespoon butter, softened
6 tablespoons whipping cream, unwhipped
1/4 cup Sugar Twin, sugar substitute, divided
1/2 teaspoon vanilla extract
dash salt
3 tablespoons water
remaining chocolate pudding mix from Cupcake recipe found on page (143)

In a small mixing bowl, beat cream cheese and butter till smooth and fluffy. Beat in unwhipped cream, Sugar Twin, vanilla extract, salt and remaining pudding mix.

Fold whipped cream into chocolate mixture. Gradually stir in water to spreading consistency.

Frost cupcakes. Best served cold!

*Makes enough frosting for 18 cupcakes. Generously!
*Frosting is 1.5 grams of carbs per serving!

Chocolate Glaze

Servings: 6

1/2 square unsweetened baking chocolate
2 tablespoons heavy cream
2 tablespoons butter, softened
1/4 cup hot water
1 1/2 teaspoons unsweetened cocoa
1/4 cup Sugar Twin, sugar substitute
1/4 teaspoon Xanthan Gum
3/4 teaspoon Equal® sweetener
1/4 teaspoon vanilla extract
water to thin glaze consistency

Melt baking chocolate and butter in small microwave-safe bowl 1-2 minutes on high, stirring every 30 seconds. Stir in hot water and set aside.

In medium bowl, mix together cocoa, Sugar Twin, Xanthan Gum and Equal sweetener. Stir in chocolate and butter mixture and vanilla extract. Beat vigorously.

Thin with water if necessary to glaze consistency.

*Makes a total of 10.6 very Chocolaty grams of carbs!

Serving Ideas: *Use on Boston Cream Pie (page 138).

Crust for Pies

1/4 cup Dr. Atkins Bake Mix
1/2 teaspoon Guar Gum
2 tablespoons Sugar Twin, sugar substitute
1/2 cup heavy cream
1 large egg
1 teaspoon vanilla extract

Pre-heat oven to 350 degrees. Whisk Bake Mix, Guar Gum and Sugar Twin together in a small mixing bowl. Whisk in cream, eggs and vanilla extract till smooth.

Let set for 10 minutes. Spread in 9" buttered pie pan. Bake @ 350 degrees for 16-18 minutes or till set and browned around edges.

Cool in pan on rack.

*Makes 1 crust recipe at a total of 9.3 grams of carbs.
Serving Ideas: *Makes a great crust for Lemon Meringue Pie (page 149)!

VARIATION:

DESSERT CRUST -
1/4 cup Dr. Atkins Bake Mix
1/2 teaspoon Guar Gum
2 tablespoons Sugar Twin, sugar substitute
3/4 cup heavy cream
2 large eggs
1 teaspoon vanilla extract
Pre-heat oven to 350 degrees. Whisk first 3 ingredients together in medium bowl. Add remaining ingredients and whisk till fairly smooth. Pour into a sprayed 9"X13" cake pan and tap on counter to level. Bake @ 350 degrees for 15-20 minutes till beginning to lightly brown. Cool in pan on rack. For thicker crust, bake in 8" square or round pan. Will need to extend bake time.
Makes 1 Dessert Crust recipe with a total of 10.3 grams of carbs!

Sweetened Whipped Cream

Servings: 12

1 cup heavy whipping cream
1/2 teaspoon vanilla extract
3 tablespoons Sugar Twin, sugar substitute
1/4 teaspoon Equal® sweetener

Whip ingredients together till thick with electric mixer. DO NOT over beat or will turn to butter.

Refrigerate till serving time.

*Recipe contains a total of 8.8 grams of carbs and only .7 grams of carbs per serving!

Serving Ideas: *Best served within 24 hours. Blend together just before serving. Use on any of your favorite dessert recipes!

VARIATION:

FROZEN WHIPPED CREAM CLOUDS - Whip together "Sweetened Whipped Cream" ingredients till thick. Line a 11"X15" jelly roll pan with waxed paper or plastic wrap. Spoon whipped cream into 12 equal mounds, shaping nicely with spoon. Make sure cream is whipped enough to hold it's shape, but take care not to whip it till it turns to butter. Place baking sheet in freezer till mounds are frozen through. Then carefully remove them and place in a lock-top plastic bag. Store in freezer. Use as needed for Orange Dream or Root Beer Floats or place frozen whipped cream clouds on any dessert and let thaw!
*Makes 12 servings @ only .7 grams of carbs per serving!

Lemon Cheesecake

Servings: 16

5 - 8 ounce packages cream cheese, softened

1/4 pound butter, softened (1 stick)

1 1/2 small boxes sugar-free lemon Jell-O (1/2 box = 1/2 T. + 1 pinch)

1/3 cup boiling water

1/2 cup whipping cream

1 teaspoon grated lemon zest, just yellow part - no white

2/3 cup Sugar Twin, sugar substitute

6 large eggs, yolks broken

Beat cream cheese and butter in large bowl with electric mixer till smooth and creamy. Dissolve Jell-O in boiling water. Takes time to dissolve completely in small amount of water. Beat Jell-O into cream cheese gradually. Add cream, Sugar Twin and lemon peel and mix till blended. Add eggs and mix on low speed ONLY TILL COMBINED. DO NOT OVERMIX.

Texture will be grainy , not creamy if you overmix the eggs. Pour into 9" sprayed springform pan. Wrap outside bottom of pan and up sides with aluminium foil. Rap pan several times on counter-top to release air bubbles.

Bake @ 325 degrees for 60-70 minutes until just set. Turn oven off and let cool inside oven for 1 hour. Finish cooling at room temperature. Do Not Remove sides of pan until completely cooled to room temperature. Cover and refrigerate at least 6 hours. Will get firmer as it chills.

*Makes 16 awesome servings @ only 3 grams of carbs per serving!

Serving Ideas:

VARIATIONS:

For ORANGE CHEESECAKE - Substitute equal amounts of orange zest and orange sugar-free Jell-O.

For LIME CHEESECAKE - Substitute equal amounts of lime zest and lime sugar-free Jell-O.

*Top with one of your favorite Berry Sauces (page 123).

Lemon Meringue Pie

Servings: 6

1 recipe *CRUST FOR PIES* (page 146)

FILLING

1 cup Sugar Twin, sugar substitute

1/8 teaspoon plus a pinch of salt

1 1/2 teaspoons Xanthan Gum

1/2 teaspoon Guar Gum

1/2 cup fresh squeezed lemon juice

1 1/2 cups cold water

1 1/2 teaspoons lemon zest grated (yellow part of lemon only)

3 large egg yolks, slightly beaten

1 tablespoon + 1 teaspoon Equal® sweetener

1 1/2 tablespoons butter

MERINGUE

4 large egg, whites

1/2 teaspoon cream of tartar

1/4 cup Sugar Twin, sugar substitute

1 teaspoon Equal® sweetener

1 teaspoon Guar Gum

1/4 teaspoon vanilla extract

Prepare crust and set aside to cool. FILLING: Mix Sugar Twin, salt, Xanthan Gum and Guar Gum in medium heavy saucepan. Whisk in lemon juice and water. Cook over medium heat stirring constantly till just beginning to boil. Briskly beat a couple of tablespoons lemon mixture into egg yolks. Then beat in another 2 tablespoons slowly. Pour yolk mixture into pan, whisking briskly and continue to cook over low heat another 5-7 minutes. Stir in lemon zest, butter and Equal sweetener. Cool a few minutes and pour into cooled pie crust.

MERINGUE: Place all meringue ingredients in a medium mixing bowl and whip till very stiff. Spread over lemon filling, make sure to seal to crust. Bake in pre-heated oven @ 400 degrees about 10 minutes.
*Makes 6 heavenly servings @ only 8 grams of carbs per serving!

Serving Ideas: *If you like pie you're gonna love this one!*

Lime Frosted Jell-O

Servings: 10

2 small packages sugar-free Jell-O, lime flavored , divided (remove 1/2 teaspoon and set aside)

1 tablespoon hot water

1 cup heavy whipping cream

1 tablespoon sugar-free instant Jell-O vanilla pudding mix

1 teaspoon lime zest, grated (green part only)

Make Jell-O with 1 3/4 cups boiling water. Stir well till dissolved then add 2 cups cold water and refrigerate till set. Dissolve 1/2 teaspoon of reserved Jell-O in 1 tablespoon hot water, set aside to cool at room temperature.

Beat remaining ingredients together, (including cooled 1/2 teaspoon Jell-O set aside to cool at room temperature) in a medium mixing bowl with an electric mixer till thick.

Spread over set Jell-O. Cut into 10 equal servings.

*Makes 10 refreshing servings @ only 1.2 grams of carbs per serving!

Old Fashioned Vanilla Pudding

1 cup heavy cream

1/2 cup water

3 large egg yolks (save the whites for pancakes)

1/4 cup Sugar Twin, sugar substitute

1 teaspoon Xanthan Gum

1/2 teaspoon vanilla extract

1/4 teaspoon almond extract

3/4 teaspoon Equal® sweetener

Heat cream and water in a medium, heavy saucepan till hot but not boiling. Skin will form on top. While cream and water are heating, beat egg yolks with a fork in small bowl just till smooth. Set aside. Mix Sugar Twin and Xanthan Gum in a separate small bowl and set aside. When cream is hot, add a small amount VERY SLOWLY, about 2-3 tablespoons to egg yolks, stirring QUICKLY with a fork. Add another 2-3 tablespoons hot cream VERY SLOWLY to egg yolks, stirring QUICKLY with a fork. Pour yolk mixture SLOWLY into remaining cream in saucepan whisking QUICKLY. Reduce heat to low and sprinkle Sugar Twin mixture gradually over pudding and whisk in till smooth. Cook for 3-4 minutes till thickened, then remove from heat. Add extracts and pour into a plastic bowl. *If mixture separates, let cool a bit and whisk till creamy. Cover with plastic wrap directly on pudding so skin won't form. Whisk in Equal sweetener after mixture has cooled. Refrigerate covered.

Makes 3 - 1/2 cup irresistible servings @ only 4.5 grams of carbs per serving!!

Serving Ideas: Makes a fabulous filling for Boston Creme Pie recipe found on page (136).

VARIATION:
CHOCOLATE PUDDING - For Chocolate Pudding add 2 tablespoons of unsweetened cocoa with the Sugar Twin mixture and omit the almond extract!
*Makes 3 - 1/2 cup servings @ only 6.5 grams of carbs per serving!

Peanut Butter & Chocolate Patties

Servings: 32

4 ounces cream cheese, softened

1/4 pound butter, softened (1 stick)

1/2 cup Skippy smooth peanut butter

5 tablespoons Sugar Twin, sugar substitute

1 teaspoon Equal® sweetener

1 teaspoon vanilla extract

Beat cream cheese in medium bowl till smooth with electric mixer. Add remaining ingredients and beat till smooth. Spread evenly in an 8" square pan, lined with waxed paper. Refrigerate till firm.

COATING:
3 T. skinless, salted peanuts, chopped very fine (Food processor works best)
3 T. plain pork rinds (0 carbs) crushed very fine in food processor
2 T. unsweetened baking cocoa
4 T. Sugar Twin, sugar substitute
1 t. Equal sweetener
1 T. sugar-free Jell-O instant Chocolate pudding mix

Mix all together in a small bowl. Set aside.

Turn out candy onto a cutting board and divide into 32 equal pieces. Shape into patties and roll in coating.

Refrigerate or freeze.

*Peanut butter mixture contains 22.3 grams of carbs total.
*Coating mixture contains 18.1 grams of carbs total.

*Makes 32 great servings @ only 1.3 grams of carbs per serving!

Pistachio Ice Cream

Servings: 12

2 1/2 cups whipping cream

1/2 cup water

1/2 cup pistachio nuts, shelled and chopped

1/2 cup Sugar Twin, sugar substitute

1 tablespoon + 1 teaspoon Equal® sweetener

1 teaspoon almond extract

8 drops green food coloring

Whisk all ingredients in medium bowl till well blended. Pour into freezer bowl of ice cream maker while running and run for about 25 minutes or till thick.

Pour into paper cups (1/2 cup into each) and freeze covered with plastic wrap.

You can thaw each serving on low in the microwave for 15 seconds.

*Makes 12 incredible servings @ only 3 grams of carbs per serving!

Serving Ideas:

*If you don't have an ice cream freezer, after whisking all ingredients together, freeze in bowl till starting to get thick. Beat with electric mixer, then pour into paper cups and cover with plastic wrap. Out of sight!!

Pumpkin Pecan Dessert

Servings: 8

3/4 cup Sugar Twin, sugar substitute

2 1/4 teaspoons ground cinnamon, divided

3/4 teaspoon ground ginger

1/4 teaspoon ground cloves

1/2 teaspoon salt

1 - 16 ounce can solid pack pumpkin

1 cup whipping cream

1/4 cup sour cream

3 large eggs, slightly beaten

1 tablespoon Brown Sugar Twin, sugar substitute

3 tablespoons toasted pecans, chopped small

Whisk together Sugar Twin, 2 teaspoons cinnamon, ginger, cloves, salt, pumpkin, whipping cream, sour cream and eggs in a medium mixing bowl till well blended.

Pour into 8 sprayed custard cups. Sprinkle top with Brown Sugar Twin, 1/4 teaspoon ground cinnamon then pecans. Bake @ 325 degrees in a pre-heated oven for 30-40 minutes or till center is almost set. Cool on a rack. Cover and chill till cold.

*Makes 8 super servings @ only 5.3 grams of carbs per serving!

Serving Ideas:
*Serve with Sweetened Whipped Cream recipe found on page (147) if desired!

Strawberry Cheesecake

Servings: 16

5 - 8 ounce packages cream cheese, softened

1/4 pound butter, softened (1 stick)

1 1/2 boxes sugar-free Strawberry Jell-O (1/2 box = 1/2 tablespoon + a pinch)

1/3 cup boiling water

1/2 cup heavy whipping cream

1 cup strawberries, chopped

3/4 cup Sugar Twin, sugar substitute

6 large eggs, yolks broken

Beat cream cheese and butter in large bowl with electric mixer till smooth and creamy. Dissolve Jell-O in boiling water. Takes time to dissolve Jell-O completely in small amount of water.

Beat Jell-O into cream cheese gradually. Add cream, Sugar Twin and strawberries, beat till well mixed. Add eggs and mix on low speed, mix ONLY till combined. DO NOT OVERMIX or texture will become grainy instead of creamy.

Spray a 9" spring form pan and wrap outside bottom and up sides with aluminum foil. Pour mixture into pan and rap several times on countertop to release air bubbles.

Bake @ 325 degrees for 60-70 minutes till just set. Turn off oven and let cool inside oven for 1 hour. Finish cooling @ room temperature. Do Not Remove sides of pan until completely cooled to room temperature. Cover and refrigerate at least 6 hours before serving. Will get firmer as it chills.

*Makes 12 servings @ 4 grams of carbs per serving. Magnificent!

Serving Ideas:
*Top with Sweetened Whipped Cream recipe (page 147) if desired!

Strawberry Crepes

Servings: 6

butter (use amount necessary to fry crepes)

3 large eggs

2/3 cup heavy cream

3 tablespoons Dr. Atkins Bake Mix

4 tablespoons Sugar Twin, sugar substitute

1/8 teaspoon almond extract

1/4 teaspoon vanilla extract

1/2 teaspoon orange zest grated (orange part only)

STRAWBERRY FILLING

2 cups strawberries, washed, hulled and sliced

6 tablespoons Sugar Twin, sugar substitute

1 recipe *Sweetened Whipped Cream (page 147)

Whisk together all crepe ingredients in a medium bowl. Melt about 1 tablespoon of butter in a heavy 8" skillet or crepe pan over medium heat.

When foam subsides, pour 1/6 of batter in pan and tilt pan to cover entire bottom evenly. Cook till lightly browned on underside and top side is set. Turn carefully and cook till other side starts to brown. Remove from pan and place between paper towels.

Repeat with remaining batter. This can be done ahead, just wrap with plastic wrap (after they have cooked) till serving time.

*STRAWBERRY FILLING: Combine strawberries and Sugar Twin and place 1/4 cup on each crepe and roll up. Place each on dessert plate. Spoon whipped cream over each crepe and garnish with rest of strawberries.

*Makes 6 delicious servings @ only 6.6 grams of carbs per serving!

Serving Ideas:
*Add an extra 2 tablespoons of Sugar Twin to whipping cream for a little more sweetness!
This makes a wonderfully light dessert or a special breakfast!

Strawberry-Kiwi Puff

Servings: 12

2 small boxes sugar-free Strawberry-Kiwi Jell-O, prepared as directed

1 1/2 cups whipping cream

1/2 teaspoon vanilla extract

3 tablespoons Sugar Twin, sugar substitute, divided

1 teaspoon sugar-free Strawberry Jell-O, dry

1 1/2 cups sliced strawberries, mixed with 1 T. of the Sugar Twin

Pour prepared Strawberry-Kiwi Jell-O into rectangular glass baking dish (8"x 11 1/2"). Refrigerate till set.

Whip cream, vanilla, 2 tablespoons Sugar Twin and dry Jell-O till very thick but soft peaks. Stir in Strawberries and spread evenly over Jell-O.

Cut into 12 equal servings.

*Makes 12 servings @ only 2.2 grams of carbs per serving!

Strawberry Snowballs

Servings: 4

"BASE LAYER"

1 cup heavy whipping cream

2 large eggs

1/2 cup water

1 tablespoon sugar-free Jell-O instant vanilla pudding mix

1 teaspoon vanilla extract

1/4 teaspoon almond extract

1 tablespoon Dr. Atkins Bake Mix

1 tablespoon Sugar Twin, sugar substitute

1/2 teaspoon Guar Gum

butter, for greasing custard cups

"STRAWBERRY LAYER"

1 cup strawberries, sliced

Sugar Twin, sugar substitute, to taste

"TOPPING"

1 1/2 cups heavy whipping cream

1 1/2 teaspoons vanilla extract

4 tablespoons Sugar Twin, sugar substitute

Pre-heat oven to 325 degrees. Butter 4 - 6 ounce custard cups or Texas size muffin cups. (Fill any empty ones with water to prevent pan from warping.) In medium bowl whisk eggs, cream and water together till well combined. Add remaining ingredients and whisk till nearly smooth. Pour into prepared pans, dividing evenly.

If using custard cups, place on a baking sheet (not insulated) and bake @ 325 degrees for 45 minutes or till set and slightly browned. Cool on rack. When cool, refrigerate till cold. Divide sweetened strawberries equally and spoon strawberry layer over each custard cup. Spread topping on top of strawberries in each custard cup and refrigerate till serving time.

TOPPING - Whip all ingredients till thickened.

*Makes 4 delicious servings @ 9 grams of carbs per serving!

INDEX

Index